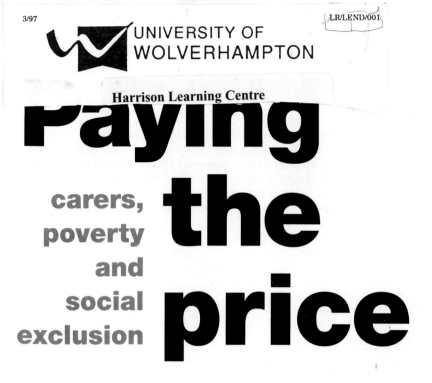

UNIVERSITY OF
WOLVERHAMPTON

Harrison Learning Centre

Paying

carers, poverty and social exclusion the price

Marilyn Howard

CPAG • 94 White Lion Street • London N1 9PF

CPAG promotes action for the relief, directly or indirectly, of poverty among children and families with children. We work to ensure that those on low incomes get their full entitlements to welfare benefits. In our campaigning and information work we seek to improve benefits and policies for low-income families in order to eradicate the injustice of poverty. If you are not already supporting us, please consider making a donation, or ask for details of our membership schemes and publications.

Poverty Publication 104

Published by CPAG
94 White Lion Street, London N1 9PF

© CPAG 2001

ISBN 1 901698 39 4

The views expressed in this book are the author's and do not necessarily express those of CPAG.

A CIP record for this book is available from the British Library

Cover and design by Devious Designs 0114 275 5634
Typeset by Boldface 020 7253 2014
Printed by Russell Press 0115 978 4505
Cover photo by Jacky Chapman/Format

With thanks to Marj for giving me an experience of caring

ACKNOWLEDGEMENTS

I would particularly like to thank Emily Holzhausen and her colleagues at Carers UK for their help and contribution to this book. Thanks go too to Gary Kitchen at Southwark Carers for generously allowing me to use their survey results. I am also grateful to Hilary Arksey and Michael Hirst, and to Saul Becker and Martin Barnes for reading the draft manuscript. I would also like to thank Alison Key for managing the book's production and to Paula McDiarmid for proofreading the text.

Marilyn Howard

ABOUT THE AUTHOR

Marilyn Howard is an independent social policy analyst, and has undertaken research and consultancy for a number of voluntary organisations, think tanks and universities, including government-commissioned evaluation. She has been an adviser to two select committees and is currently a member of the Disability Living Allowance Advisory Board. She has also worked as a probation officer, welfare rights adviser and community social worker. She writes here in a personal capacity.

CONTENTS

GLOSSARY

AA	Attendance allowance
AMLs	Activities involved in managing life
BHPS	British Household Panel Survey
CTB	Council tax benefit
DfEE	Department for Education and Employment
DLA	Disability living allowance
DoH	Department of Health
DPTC	Disabled person's tax credit
DSS	Department of Social Security
DTI	Department of Trade and Industry
DWP	Department for Work and Pensions
ETC	Employment tax credit
ETU	Earnings top-up
EU	European Union
GHS	General Household Survey
HB	Housing benefit
ICA	Invalid care allowance
ICT	Information and communication technology
ILA	Individual learning account
IS	Income support
IT	Information technology
JSA	Jobseeker's allowance
S2P	State second pension
SDP	Severe disability premium
SERPS	State earnings-related pension
SPRU	Social Policy Research Unit, York University
SSI	Social Services Inspectorate
WFTC	Working families' tax credit

FOREWORD

In my daily contact with carers, I am struck by how frequently they tell me about the financial impact of caring on their household. Everyone can be affected and, as some of Carers UK's earlier research has shown, carers and their families can experience lasting poverty as a result of the costs of caring.

Caring is not something that happens to others. Three out of five of us will have caring responsibilities at some point during our lifetime. Nor is caring necessarily an isolated incident. We may end up caring several times throughout our life. None of us should be complacent about the impact of caring. As this study shows, caring affects your work, your ability to care safely, your health and well-being and your quality of life. This is not least because the costs of disability and caring are considerable in terms of both direct costs and opportunity costs. The costs of caring spread beyond the carer, affecting other members of the close family, particularly children.

No two caring situations are the same, so a range of sensitive and well-targeted measures are needed to ensure that carers and their families avoid and are lifted out of lasting poverty and social exclusion. Marilyn Howard's work takes this broad perspective, examining the many different pressures on carers that may result in financial hardship and limit their social inclusion. This joint piece of work also looks at different income issues from a range of carers' perspectives; from younger carers aged 16, to older carers, and those from minority ethnic communities.

As this work highlights, while a number of positive steps have been taken by the Government to tackle carers' social exclusion and financial difficulties, there is still much more to do. Looking ahead, the economic and social imperative to support carers will only increase as our population ages. In the next 30 years, unless support services increase dramatically, the pressure to care for our elderly, chronically ill or disabled relatives and friends will rise considerably. The time for action, however, is now if we are to ensure that carers have the freedom and choice to maximise their opportunities in life, and are able to continue caring (if they chose to) safely and without severe financial penalties.

Action is not simply the preserve of the UK Government, although there is much more that it could do to build on its support for carers. We need employers, the NHS, the devolved parliaments and assemblies, local authorities, service providers and the voluntary sector to work together to recognise and support carers. All of us have an interest both as individuals and as organisations in ensuring a more secure future for carers.

Finally, this report would not have been possible without the financial support of the Alzheimer's Society and the enthusiasm of the Child Poverty Action Group. We are very grateful for their support and commitment to improving the lot of carers.

Diana Whitworth
Chief Executive, Carers UK

Introduction

THE CONTEXT

A carer is someone who provides support to an elderly, ill or disabled person (often a relative) who cannot manage alone without assistance. The support carers give is unpaid.

The work of such carers is thought to save the taxpayer an estimated £34 billion in health and social services.[1] Yet many carers are living in poverty, excluded from social activities and paid employment, often feeling isolated and unrecognised in their role.

This book brings together some of the experiences of carers, using previously unpublished material from Carers UK (previously the Carers National Association) as well as other published research. Issues needing further consideration, and recommendations, are highlighted in the text and summarised in Chapter 12.

While there have been a number of positive government initiatives, the depth and extent of poverty and social exclusion among carers means that more may be needed to ensure that those who provide care to others continue to do so.

GOVERNMENT INITIATIVES

The 1997–2001 Parliament saw some progress in supporting carers. A National Strategy for Carers was launched for England in 1998, and a year later, £140 million was allocated to English local authorities to provide respite care over three years. In September 2000 the Government announced that the Carers Special Grant for English local authorities would be doubled by 2003/04.[2] With the implementation of the Carers and Disabled Children Act 2000, carers can now have an assessment in their own right, undertaken by social services departments in England and Wales. There is now a website for and about carers, and 'looking after someone' is one of the life episodes appearing in the new UK Online website.

Carers can now benefit from time off work for family emergencies and are included in second-tier pension reform. Above-inflation increases in carers' benefits took place in April 2001, with further improvements planned, including changing the name of invalid care allowance to carer's allowance. These changes are due to help an estimated 300,000 carers at a cost of £500 million over three years.[3]

DEMAND AND SUPPLY OF CARE

It is difficult to predict the implications of trends in caring, but it is likely that there will be a bigger *demand* for care in the future. People are now living longer than ever before, and it is estimated that by 2021 there will be 11 million people over age 65, some two million more than in 1997; by 2025 the number of over-90s is expected to double.[4] Older people are more likely to develop ill-health or disability, particularly in the over-75 age group.[5] More people seem to prefer to remain in their own homes when becoming more frail or disabled. As the elderly population grows, so does the likelihood that rising numbers will require assistance with daily tasks. Already eight out of ten elderly people who have help with domestic tasks rely on care from relatives and neighbours and fewer elderly people are receiving home care from social services.[6] The health of those near retirement age – the 55-64 age group – will also affect demand for care into this century, and it is expected that this group may have a longer, but not necessarily healthier, retirement.[7]

At the same time, people still expect that others will provide care for them. Research for Carers UK found that 63 per cent of people who were not current carers expected that family or friends would look after them (although most thought the state should pay), and few expected help from health or social services.[8] Given these trends, it is likely that the need for care will grow.

However, willingness to *supply* care is uncertain. There is evidence of some continued willingness to provide care, although women were more prepared to be carers than men.[9] A study for Carers UK predicted a reduced supply of carers in the future, especially for 'co-resident' care, due to:

- more (married) women working full time, which both decreases the likelihood of caring and the number of hours spent caring;
- higher levels of educational attainment (having a similar effect as full-time employment);
- a reduction in the married population, as well as higher divorce rates, which might reduce the provision of care by people in the same household;
- higher levels of owner occupation (perhaps indicating households with more wealth).[10]

On the other hand, some people aged 60-75 are fit, may want more opportunities to work, and may also be encouraged to offer care as part of their continuing contribution to society.[11]

Overall, the trends suggest that there may be a shortfall in the amount of care needed; if so, there is a danger that more disabled and older people might require more intensive formal care, including residential care. This could be more costly to the individuals as well as to the state.

Incentives may well be needed to maintain current levels of care. This would suggest two objectives for policy – encouraging care as well as preventing social exclusion once someone is a carer.

WHO CARES?

Britain has an estimated 5.7 million carers; some 15 per cent of adults over 16 provide care, with about 1.7 million doing so for more than 20 hours a week, and 855,000 for more than 50 hours.[12] Of these, 459,000 are over the age of 65. The Government's large-scale *Family Resources Survey* includes information about carers, showing that in 1999/2000:

- 58 per cent provide care to someone outside the household ('extra-resident' carers); men are more likely to care for a spouse or partner, women more likely to care for a relative outside of the household;
- 8 per cent of carers look after more than one person;
- 32 per cent of adult carers are in full-time employment, compared with 45 per cent of adults; 17 per cent of carers are working part time, compared with 14 per cent of all adults;
- 22 per cent of carers are retired;

- 35 per cent of carers live in households where the main source of income is social security benefits or retirement pension; this proportion is larger as the number of hours spent caring increase.[13]

One in four carers have been caring for ten years or more and a similar proportion for between five and ten years.[14] An analysis of the British Household Panel Survey has also shown that there is also considerable stopping and starting of periods of caring, as well as longer-term periods spent caring (transitions into and out of caring are discussed in Chapter 4):

- More than a third of carers start or end care-giving each year and over half are replaced by another 'cohort' of carers every five years.[15]

SUBSTANTIAL CARING

Distinctions are often made between 'helping' and 'substantial' caring.[16] Substantial involvement can be defined either by:

- the number of hours (where 20 hours per week is normally taken as the threshold); *or*
- whether the care is for someone in the same household (co-resident care); *or*
- the patterns of caring activity (tasks like helping with personal and/or physical care might be used as a measure of substantial care).

Over a million carers are involved in providing substantial amounts of care, and the proportion of carers doing so has increased since 1993, coinciding with the implementation of community care legislation.[17]

'Turnover' is also high among substantial carers. The Social Policy Research Unit (SPRU) at York University has found that two-thirds of people caring for someone in the same household (co-resident carers) were not caring five years earlier, and three-quarters of those caring for more than 20 hours a week were not doing so five years earlier. Three in ten carers were co-resident and one in five spent 20 hours or more each week in caring activities – equivalent to 40–53 households per 1,000.[18] Table 1.1 shows the estimated numbers of people starting, continuing and ending a period of caring.

TABLE 1.1 **Annual estimates of numbers of people providing substantial care**

20 or more hours a week	Local authority area	Benefits Agency district office	General practice partnership	Medium sized employer
Starting	3,300	1,200	60	9
Continuing	4,000	1,450	70	6
Ceasing	2,950	1,050	55	7
No. adults	250,000	90,000	4,500	1,000

Source: M Hirst and S Hutton, 'Informal Care Over Time', *Benefits* 28, April/May 2000

CARING ACTIVITIES

One analysis of other official statistics, the General Household Survey, identified six types of caring activities:

• Personal and physical care.
• Personal not physical.
• Physical not personal.
• Other practical help.
• Practical help only.
• Other help.[19]

This analysis indicated an association between the activities involved in caring and the relationship between the carer and cared-for person:

• People helping those who were not close blood relatives were unlikely to be giving *personal or physical* types of assistance, but were more likely to provide *practical help*.
• Those helping spouses or children were more likely to be giving *personal care*.
• Those helping parents were more likely to give *physical not personal care*, or *other practical help*.

Those giving *personal and physical* care were more likely to have sole responsibility for caring for someone (70 per cent) compared with those providing *other practical help* only (of whom 52 per cent had sole responsibility).

A comparison of three different years of the General Household Survey (1985, 1990 and 1995) showed an increasing divide between the least and most involved carers: the proportions providing *personal and physical care* grew from 12 per cent in 1985 to 16 per cent in 1995.[20]

TYPES OF CARERS AND CARING RELATIONSHIPS

Carers are not a homogenous group. Chapters 5 to 8 will explore the situations of some kinds of caring relationships in more detail. These are young carers, parent carers, working-age carers and those over pension age.

Cutting across these dimensions are issues of gender, race, and some of the additional issues involved in caring for someone with mental distress. These issues are briefly taken in turn below.

GENDER

Overall, women are slightly more likely than men to be carers.[21] An estimated 42 per cent of carers are men.[22] During the 1990s, there was an increase in the proportion of both men and women providing care within the same household. More men than women took on the role of caring for their spouse, and more women than men withdrew from the less intensive care-giving between households (ie, extra-resident care).[23]

Qualitative research by Sheffield University into men without work revealed that part of the process of becoming detached from the labour market included taking on the care of a sick or disabled person in the household.[24] Often this involved caring for a spouse (who was perhaps developing mental distress) but sometimes a disabled child. Quantitative work in the same series also found that the minority of workless men who described themselves as 'full-time carers' tended to be poorly qualified and lived predominantly in rented housing, with around half having dependent children. They were more likely than men who described themselves as 'unemployed', to have left their last job voluntarily and have been out of work longer (half for five years or more). The authors speculate that had their earning power been greater, they would have remained in employment and bought in the caring services which they themselves now provided.[25] Other research for Carers UK also suggests that formerly unemployed co-resident male carers were least likely to rejoin the labour force after caring.[26]

Men may be less easy to identify as carers, and less likely to use support services. A survey of carers' centres across the UK, carried out by Southwark Carers in June 2001, found that centres had a lower proportion of male members (on average 25 per cent) than the national average (42 per cent). Most of the centres believed that men were less likely to identify themselves as carers than women, and that the support needs of male carers might differ from those of female carers. Although small scale, this survey suggests that a disproportionate number of 'hidden carers' could be male.

MINORITY ETHNIC CARERS

The poor health experiences of people from minority ethnic groups suggest that there is likely to be a greater need for care among these communities. For instance, they have tended to be more likely than the general population to live in deprived areas; be poor; suffer ill-health and live in overcrowded and unpopular housing.[27] Their socio-economic status, associated with the processes of migration and discrimination, may also have a bearing on the differences in health.[28] As well as these factors, some conditions seem more common in different ethnic groups; for instance, it has been suggested that the prevalence of learning difficulties in people of South Asian origin could be three times higher than in other communities.[29] In London, people of Pakistani origin aged 60 and over have the highest rates of long-term limiting illness of any group, and some conditions, such as TB, affect disproportionate numbers of asylum seekers and refugees. Mental ill-health also varies across ethnic groups, for example, depression appears more common in African-Caribbeans than Whites,[30] and African-Caribbean women have higher rates of diagnosis of psychotic conditions relative to the White population.[31]

It is possible that minority ethnic carers may be more likely to be caring for more than one person at a time; of South Asian families containing someone with a learning difficulty, almost one in five have more than one member with a learning difficulty.[32]

Service provision has tended to be worse for disabled people and carers from minority ethnic groups, largely as a result of stereotypes of 'caring extended families' and assumptions of 'low numbers' of minority ethnic clients.[33] On the contrary, it has been suggested that the traditional extended family structure of South Asian families has been modified through inappropriate housing, occupational mobility and immigration policies, having an adverse effect on the ability of families to provide significant levels of support to South Asian parents of disabled children.[34]

The situation for carers from minority ethnic communities can be far worse than for White carers, as a result of high levels of unmet needs, poverty, poor housing, social isolation and lack of support, lack of information and culturally appropriate services[35] (see also Chapter 2).

CARING FOR SOMEONE WITH MENTAL DISTRESS

Most carers are looking after someone with a physical impairment, though a significant proportion have mental health problems (see Table 1.2 below).

One in four people experience mental distress at some time, and almost 1 per cent of the population has a diagnosis of manic depression or schizophrenia. Harassment, racism and bullying can be major causes of mental distress, and people who have had psychiatric treatment may find themselves targets of it.[36] The stigma associated with mental distress can lead to discrimination and social exclusion, and people may avoid services for this reason. Services can also be inappropriate or labelling; even where diagnosis leads to effective treatment of symptoms, stigma and discrimination continue.[37]

Carers do not necessarily undertake the same physical tasks for someone in mental distress as they might for someone with a physical impairment; but caring can involve offering support and encouragement as well as dealing with officials, helping with finances and often supervising medication.[38] Mental distress can often be intermittent, and this is reflected in the type of care needed; the need to be available

---

TABLE 1.2: **Impairment and household percentage, Great Britain**

Disabled person's impairment	Carer in same household	Carer in another household	Total
Physical only	66	57	60
Mental only	7	7	7
Physical and mental	22	12	15
Old age	5	23	17
Other	0	1	1

Source: derived from General Household Survey 1995, as in House of Commons, *Hansard*, 25 May 2000, col 589w

to provide care can disrupt a carer's employment patterns, routines, family life and leisure time.

Services may not always be available, and some carers can encounter difficulty in getting professionals, such as GPs, to intervene when someone's behaviour begins to deteriorate; professional help for carers may be refused or may not be available when crises occur outside usual working hours.[39] Studies have shown that families who contributed willingly to the care of people with mental distress have often felt they may have taken on too much or are unsupported – hence the need to involve patients, service users and carers in service delivery.[40]

Witnesses to the Mind inquiry into social exclusion and mental health issues also drew attention to the ways in which social exclusion could also affect carers:

> '[Carers] become ashamed, they won't talk to their friends and relatives so they lose their natural support systems. They stop inviting people into their home, and they stop taking the ill person out, so they become isolated in their own little castle. One way to address this is relatives' support groups, but these are very, very rare within the NHS.'
> (Julian Leff, Institute of Psychiatry)[41]

This chapter has highlighted some of the different kinds of relationships and factors which might affect caring. The next chapter focuses on one of the most common experiences of all carers living on a low income and incurring additional expense relating to the impairment of the cared-for person – the experience of poverty.

NOTES

1 Nuttall et al, 'Financing Long-Term Care in Great Britain', *Journal of Institute of Actuaries*, 1994

2 House of Commons, *Hansard*, 6 November 2000, col 68w

3 House of Commons, *Hansard*, 13 November 2000, col 518w; see also *Changes to Invalid Care Allowance*, A consultation paper issued by the DWP, July 2001

4 J Matheson and C Summerfield (eds), *Social Focus on Older People*, Office for National Statistics, 1999

5 Though the precise trends depend on the methodology used: this is further discussed in E Grundy et al, *Disability in Great Britain*, DSS Research Report 94, 1999

6 L Pickard, 'Policy Options for Carers of Elderly People', in *With Respect to Old Age: research vol 3*, report by the Royal Commission on Long-Term Care, Cm 4192-II/3, 1999

7 K Dunnell and D Dix, 'Are We Looking Forward to a Longer and Healthier Retirement?' *Health Statistics Quarterly*, The Stationery Office, Summer 2000

8 Report for Carers National Association by Boots the Chemist, *Who Cares? Perceptions of caring and carers*, CNA, 1996

9 See note 8

10 London Economics, *The Economics of Informal Care: a report by London Economics for Carers National Association*, 1998

11 C Glendinning and E McLaughlin, *Paying for Care: lessons from Europe*, Social Security Advisory Committee Research Report 5, HMSO, 1993

12 O Rowlands and G Parker, *Informal Carers: results of an independent study carried out by the Office for National Statistics on behalf of the Department of Health as part of the 1995 General Household Survey*, National Statistics, 1998

13 Department of Social Security, *Family Resources Survey*, Great Britain, 1999/2000, 2001

14 See note 12

15 Social Policy Research Unit, 'Informal Carers: a moving target', *Cash and Care*, Winter 1999

16 See note 6

17 See note 15

18 See note 15

19 G Parker and D Lawton, *Different Types of Care, Different Types of Carer: evidence from the General Household Survey*, SPRU/The Stationery Office, 1994

20 See note 12

21 See note 12

22 HM Government, *Caring about Carers: a national strategy for carers*, 1999

23 M Hirst, 'Trends in Informal Care in Great Britain During the 1990s', *Health and Social Care in the Community*, 2001

24 S Yeandle, *Personal Histories: the context for joblessness, disability and retirement*, Centre for Regional Economic and Social Research, Sheffield Hallam University, 1999

25 C Beatty and S Fothergill, *The Detached Male Workforce*, Centre for Regional Economic and Social Research, Sheffield Hallam University, 1999

26 See note 10

27 See for example, Social Exclusion Unit, *Minority Ethnic Issues in Social Exclusion and Neighbourhood Renewal*, Cabinet Office, 2000

28 J Nazroo, *Ethnicity and Mental Health*, Policy Studies Institute, 1997

29 South Asians between the age of 5 and 32: see G Mir et al, *Learning Difficulties and Ethnicity*, Department of Health, March 2001

30 D Acheson, *Independent Inquiry into Inequalities in Health*, The Stationery Office, 1998

31 See note 28

32 G Mir et al, *Learning Difficulties and Ethnicity*, Department of Health, March 2001

33 W I U Ahmad, *Ethnicity, Disability and Chronic Illness*, OUP, 2000

34 W Ahmad and K Atkin, *'Race' and Community Care*, OUP, 1996

35 See for example, C Ward, *Family Matters: counting families in*, Department of Health, March 2001

36 A Cobb, *Managing for Mental Health: the Mind employers' resource pack*, Mind, 2000

37 Mind, *Creating Accepting Communities: report of the Mind inquiry into social exclusion and mental health problems*, 1999

38 K Harvey, 'Being a Carer', in *Mental Illness: a handbook for carers*, Jessica Kingsley, 2001

39 See for example, G Howe, *Mental Health Assessments*, Jessica Kingsley, 1999

40 Studies referred to in Department of Health, *Modernising Mental Health Services: safe, sound and supportive*, 1998

41 See note 37

2 Carers and poverty

From a survey of carers, it was revealed that:

- one in five carers was cutting back on food;
- almost one in three had trouble paying household bills and had experienced debt;
- almost six out of ten had given up work to care, and four in five carers believed they were worse off financially since becoming a carer;
- two-thirds attributed their financial difficulties to the additional costs of disability;
- nearly four out of five found the level of charges for services caused financial difficulties;
- more than two in three carers worried most, or all, of the time about their finances;
- two in three carers believed that this worry affected their health.[1]

THE POOR CARE MORE?

As noted in Chapter 1, carers are those who provide unpaid support to disabled or elderly people who need assistance.

As people on low incomes are more likely to have poor health, it is not surprising that carers providing a substantial amount of care are also predominantly on low incomes. Though carers are drawn from all classes, one study in the early 1990s showed that looking after someone in the same household (co-resident care) – which places more constraints on a carer's life – was more frequently provided by people from lower socio-economic groups.[2] More recent data also confirms that people from manual social classes and pensioner couples on low incomes are disproportionately likely to take on a caring role.[3]

An econometric study suggests that the decision to provide care (rather than purchase it) may depend on the wages someone may be able to command in the labour market as well as feelings of love or duty.[4] Equally, the effects of ill-health of one member of a couple may not only reduce that person's participation in the labour market but have an indirect effect on the work availability of the caring spouse (see also Chapters 3 and 7).

Probably those on lower incomes bear the greatest risks with fewest resources, fewer work opportunities, poorer financial position, less leverage in purchasing substitute care, equipment and adaptations, and in negotiating with welfare professionals.

The Poverty and Social Exclusion Survey, published in 2000, showed that, compared with all children, those living with a parent or household member with poor health or a disability were a third more likely to lack basic necessities because the household could not afford them.[5]

An extensive survey of low-income families in Britain, published in 2001, also reveals an increase in numbers of families out of work during the 1990s because of ill-health/disability and caring responsibilities:

- Between 1991 and 1999, the proportion of non-working couples where the respondent cared for a disabled child *almost quadrupled*, and those caring for a disabled adult *doubled* (from 13 per cent to 26 per cent).[6]

Surprisingly, though, one analysis does not appear to have found a strong immediate impact of caring on employment (or incomes).[7] This might, however, have neglected the longer-term impact of caring; a subsequent analysis has suggested that, as periods of providing care lengthen and intensify, carers are more likely to withdraw from paid employment.[8]

Carers tended to have lower incomes in the year after caring ended, and being a carer also increased spells of unemployment among previously unemployed men (see also Chapter 4).[9] However, women beginning to provide care for another person in their own home (co-resident care) appeared to be more likely to be in employment. Women providing care to someone outside of the household (extra-resident care) were less likely to be in work. Possibly if the spouse had given up work for reasons of ill-health or disability it might be important (initially at least) for the carer to work to provide an income.

THE FINANCIAL IMPACT OF CARING

There is overwhelming evidence associating caring with financial hardship. However, while comparisons between carers and non-carers (such as by employment status and income) reveal differences, it is not always clear whether these are the result of caring or whether some are factors which determine whether or not a particular individual *becomes* a carer.[10] A recent analysis of the British Household Panel Survey does suggest, however, that longer episodes of caring lead to a widening gap in income from earnings between carers and similar non-carers.[11]

POOR MEN AND WOMEN

Carers UK (previously Carers National Association) undertook a survey of carers in 2000.[12] Although not representative of all carers, it indicated that men and women had given up work to care in similar proportions, and that their financial circumstances had worsened since becoming a carer. The differences were that:

- female carers were more likely to have trouble paying utility bills, unable to afford essential repairs and more likely to ask friends or family for financial help;
- male carers were more likely to have been in debt and to have spent income or savings on alternative care.

Male carers were:

- slightly more likely to receive income support (33 per cent compared with 28 per cent of female carers); *and*
- more likely to receive housing or council tax benefit (51 per cent compared with 46 per cent of female carers).

Equal numbers of men and women received invalid care allowance.

POOR MINORITY ETHNIC CARERS

Carers from minority ethnic groups are likely to be worse off than their White counterparts, having limited access to financial resources because of low pay, minimal pension rights or being less likely to qualify for benefits because of residence status.[13] Ethnic origin has also been considered a significant factor in the greater poverty, lack of service provision and access to benefits for parents with disabled children[14] (see also Chapter 6).

Carers UK's *Caring on the Breadline* survey included a small sample of carers from different ethnic groups (80 in number).[15] The results show greater financial hardship than the sample as a whole:

- More carers from minority ethnic groups had problems paying utility bills (54 per cent) than the sample as a whole (35 per cent) and were more likely to worry about their financial circumstances.
- Forty-six per cent of Black British/European carers and 42 per cent from other ethnic groups were, or had been, in debt compared with 34 per cent of all carers.
- Black British/European carers were more likely to have given up work to provide care (67 per cent) than all carers (59 per cent).
- Black British/European carers were more likely to find that benefits did not cover the cost of disability (67 per cent) compared with all carers (53 per cent).

MAKING ENDS MEET

Often, carers and their families have had to devise strategies to make ends meet. Many carers told Carers UK:

'We now have a strict budget to survive and pay debts. All activities are based at home. Cheap brands used for all products. We have a completely different lifestyle now. We have no spare money for redecoration, repairs, clothing or entertainment. We have less freedom in society due to financial constraints.'[16]

'I live in dread of the postman – I cannot afford essential services, especially water.'[17]

Sometimes people in mental distress can find it difficult to budget and so carers may need to assist, perhaps also lending money or paying themselves.

CUTTING BACK

In some cases, carers may neglect their own needs. Some carers reduced spending on themselves, with 64 per cent of respondents to the Carers UK survey spending less on clothes.[18]

'I have not bought myself any decent new clothes for the past three years. The charity shops have been a safe haven.'[19]

Over three-quarters of carers gave up holidays or leisure pursuits because of their caring responsibilities.[20] In this particular survey the primary reason for giving up holidays and leisure pursuits was cost.

'We have not had a proper holiday for six years. We cannot treat our children as outings are so expensive.'[21]

The opportunity to resolve any debt problems is much reduced in the absence of an income from employment.[22] One carer told Carers UK:

'I had saved for a holiday that I felt I really needed. However, since being a carer I have spent all the savings on the mortgage. Without my wages I am now in debt.'[23]

LACK OF SAVINGS

The General Household Survey analysis of matched carers and non-carers found that carers in the same household as the disabled person, and those providing the most substantial forms of care, were far less likely than their non-carer equivalents to have income from savings.[24] As age and gender were already controlled for, this is likely to be a real 'carer-effect'. Years of caring are likely to have depressed the ability to save, combined with having to spend more to meet some of the costs of disability. Those who become carers in middle age may also be propelled into an early 'old age', using up savings that they would otherwise not have touched until retirement. This has serious knock-on implications for carers' standards of living in old age (see also Chapter 8).

The *Caring on the Breadline* survey also found that nearly one in three carers had no savings at all, and of those who did, 31 per cent had less than £1,000.[25]

'I am using my savings and investments for ordinary living expenses.'[26]

Many carers also ran down their savings through paying for alternative care (see Chapters 3 and 7).

Carers are unlikely to have the opportunity to put aside amounts on a regular basis for savings, often because they are not in employment or are living on low fixed incomes after retirement,

and because of the high costs of disability, which they share. The Government's proposals to encourage more people to save on a regular basis (such as the Child Trust Fund and the Savings Gateway for adults) need to be sufficiently flexible to enable carers to save when they can, perhaps only intermittently, without incurring financial penalty.[27]

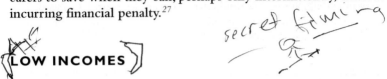

LOW INCOMES

Many carers are on low, fixed incomes. Carers are rarely separately identified in income statistics, but households with a disabled member (which may also contain carers) tend to be in the bottom 40 per cent of incomes.[28] Working-age households with both a disabled adult and child were more at risk of a low income, with over 70 per cent in the bottom two-fifths of the income distribution.

In one study of carers in the mid-1990s, households containing carers were clustered in the bottom two-fifths of income distribution.[29] The General Household Survey analysis referred to above matched carers and non-carers by characteristics such as age and gender. This found that the average personal income of female carers was little different from non-carers (perhaps reflecting the lower incomes of women generally). Yet for males there was a significant difference (£12 a week in 1985, representing about £22 today), and was especially high for same-household carers (£15 then, perhaps £28 today).[30] Caring for someone in another household seemed to make less difference. Further 'matched' research would be needed to explore whether this gap remains.

LOSS OF EARNINGS

Low incomes are often the result of carers having to reduce their hours of work or give up paid employment altogether. The matched General Household Survey analysis also found that:

● carers providing personal and physical care had reduced earnings (because they were less likely to be in work), as did those providing physical not personal care and other practical help (because they were more likely to be in part-time work). Carers had lower earnings than matched non-carers, reflecting the lower frequency of part-time work, but for non-resident carers earnings were only slightly lower.[31]

Carers UK research has also revealed that 77 per cent of carers felt themselves to be worse off financially since they began caring, and over seven in ten had given up work to provide care:

> 'I gave up a £25K pa job to care. I received no help with my mortgage or other bills; just ICA [invalid care allowance], less than £40 a week. I had to buy a bigger car for the wheelchair, to attend appointments – no travel allowance.' (Female carer under 40)[32]

CARERS PROVIDING SUBSTANTIAL SUPPORT

Most carers looking after someone for more than 35 hours a week are predominantly on very low incomes, half receiving less than £50 a week before benefits, as Table 2.1 below reveals.

TABLE 2.1: **Numbers of carers[33] by weekly household equivalised net income (excluding benefits) below the given thresholds in 1997/98**

Weekly income	Before housing costs	After housing costs
Less than £50	410,000 (52%)	450,000 (56%)
£50 – £100	90,000 (11%)	80,000 (10%)
£100 – £150	80,000 (10%)	90,000 (11%)
£150 – £200	80,000 (10%)	60,000 (8%)
Above £200	130,000 (17%)	120,000 (15%)
Total	800,000 (100%)	800,000 (100%)

Source: House of Lords, *Hansard*, 28 October 1999, col WA 46

HOUSEHOLDS RELIANT ON BENEFITS

Many carers (especially those with substantial caring responsibilities) rely on social security benefits for their income, and live in households where the main source of income is disability or other benefits.[34] The General Household Survey matched analysis also found that, among male carers and those providing practical help only, receipt of invalidity benefit (the predecessor of incapacity benefit) was high.[35] This, they

suggest, could be due to male carers negotiating a 'sick role' to provide care or who might have been able to take on limited amounts of caring activity if they left the labour market. Alternatively, people who are more disadvantaged in the labour market could be more likely to take on a caring role (see Chapter 1).

The British Household Panel Survey analysis also showed that receipt of invalid care allowance (ICA) increased with longer periods of providing care, though there appeared to be no clear trend over time for receipt of means-tested benefits to increase.[36]

THE EXTRA COSTS ASSOCIATED WITH CARING

As well as having low incomes, carers often incur extra expenses. Carers UK's recent *Caring on the Breadline* survey showed that 64 per cent of carers said they faced extra costs because of the additional expense associated with disability.[37] One in three carers had problems paying bills for gas, electricity, telephone, etc. One carer told Carers UK:

> 'My husband is now incontinent. My electric and water and gas bills have increased, ie lights are on all night, extra washing (clothes) extra baths.'[38]

Often these costs, such as for heating, laundry, etc, had to be met from the household – ie, from *both* the disabled person and the carer.

WHOSE COSTS?

While the extra expenses incurred in such items may be met by the carer, particularly for co-resident carers, there are differences of view between the disability movement and academics about whose costs they are. The former argue that these are disability costs which should be met through better disability benefits, the latter that they are expenses born by carers and are an additional argument for increasing support such as ICA.[39] The distinction that has been made is that:

- *disability costs* consist of housing, heating, laundry, clothing, bedding, toiletries (which can fall on the carer because of the inadequacy of disability benefits), as well as formal personal assistance; whereas
- *carer costs* can include transport,[40] adapting the carer's home, costs arising from the carer's lack of time (eg, convenience foods, car for

shopping, cleaning and replacement of a carer's clothes and a phone to keep in touch).

However, research has also revealed caring relationships as a two-way process, with the carer and disabled person complementing each other.[41] Disabled people contribute towards household tasks and child-care, rarely doing nothing at all. Commentators have also emphasised the reciprocity and independence in relationships, rather than caring simply being a one-way process where the carer gives and the cared-for receives; disabled people do not stop functioning as parents/relatives, nor stop caring about or for others.

> 'This term 'carer' is not a nice one, because there's this shift in power. I don't like the term 'carer'. It removes the interdependence. It immediately becomes not a relationship any more. A relationship is about balance, isn't it?'[42]

Here the view is taken that most of the additional expenses should be properly regarded as a disability-related cost – and so could be tackled via improvements to disabled people's incomes (see especially substitute care while at work in Chapter 7).

MONEY TRANSFERS BETWEEN DISABLED PEOPLE AND CARERS

There is little information about how disabled people and carers handle their finances, or any conflicts between them. However, anecdotal information suggests that there may be complex interactions, and that there can be power imbalances in either direction. Research conducted in the late 1980s indicated that the household distribution between disabled people and carers could reflect patterns of budgeting established before caring began (such as with spouse carers), the capacity of the disabled person to manage their own financial affairs, and the household status of the disabled person.[43] The most common form of budgeting in that small-scale study involved *carer control*, followed by *joint control* and then *separate control*. Conflicts were less widespread than the authors had anticipated, affecting one in five carers, who reported some difficulties in getting cash from the cared-for person, but also some carer reluctance to take over the financial affairs of the disabled person. However, the same research indicated tensions generated by the formal status required for benefit purposes (such as non-dependant deductions and implications for household finances overall). More extensive research would be needed to explore money transfers between disabled people and carers in the present context.

There is anecdotal evidence of similar tensions today with regard to the overlap between the carer's ICA and the disabled person's severe disability premium (see Chapter 9).

Financial independence can also be an issue for young disabled people in their transition into adulthood. For instance, disability benefits paid for a young disabled person are rarely under her or his control, and her/his financial status is often 'negotiated' with her/his parents.[44] Indeed, the greatest boost to financial independence is earning a wage – highlighting the importance of access to employment for young disabled people.

The sensitivity of these issues needs to be borne in mind when policy options are being considered. It is possible that, for example, some disabled people prefer to retain control via the employment relationship rather than care. If paid care is considered to be a disability-related cost, then this needs to be firmly under the control of the disabled person.

This then raises the question of whether all payments for care should be channelled through the disabled person, in effect making all care 'formal'. The arguments in favour of an income independent of the disabled person for carers revolve around retaining an incentive to provide care without financial penalty. This may become important if some incentives are necessary to maintain the supply of unpaid care at a time when the demand for carers is likely to increase.

It has been said that factors which transform an impairment into a disability also tend to transform family members and friends into 'carers'.[45] Hence, better support services, well-designed toilets and bathrooms and accessible transport may change the demand for some forms of care.

In the meantime, there are costs such as transport and council tax, where concessions could be extended as a way of reducing some of the expenses which can, in practice, be borne by carers.

TRANSPORT

Transport can be a major expense for carers, especially extra-resident carers. Carers told Carers UK:

'The person being cared for does not go out but the carer must go for them – so some help with transport costs.'

'Also petrol prices, we are in a rural area totally dependent on a car.'[46]

Exemption from vehicle excise duty is available to disabled drivers who receive the higher rate of disability living allowance mobility component. Technically a car is now only exempt when being used solely by, or for the purposes of, the disabled person; other usage could lead to prosecution.[47] Although it could be argued that a carer's use of the vehicle in connection with their caring role could fall within the scope of this provision, carers may be reluctant to rely on the goodwill of transport authorities in this regard.

There should be some recognition of the transport costs incurred by carers. Either the disabled passengers scheme could be reinstated, or a reduced level of road tax introduced for carers (unless the vehicle is already exempt). The latter could be triggered by entitlement to ICA or the carer premium. Local transport concessions could be extended to include ICA/carer premium/or someone who has been assessed by her/his social services department as a carer.

HOUSEHOLD EQUIPMENT

In the matched General Household Survey sample, carers were more likely to own washing machines (male and female carers) and cars (only female carers) than non-carers.[48] However, it was carers giving *other practical help*, or living in different households, who were more likely to have cars and washing machines. House repairs and maintenance may be neglected because of cost; 40 per cent of carers responding to the *Caring on the Breadline* survey said they could not afford essential repairs to their home.[49]

'Wear and tear on furnishings is higher than normal; one has to buy durable, practical, hard-wearing all the time. This takes money.'[50]

Unless caring for a disabled child, there is no access to help with key items like washing machines (such as from the Family Fund)[51] unless via the social fund:

- *The regulated social fund* provides lump-sum payments for contingencies such as maternity and funeral expenses and cold weather. Winter fuel payments are also made through this system.

- *Community care grants*, part of the discretionary cash-limited social fund, are grants for people receiving income support with limited savings, for the purpose of easing 'exceptional' family pressures or promoting community care (or preventing institutionalisation). Certain items are excluded, such as daily living expenses, fuel costs, medical items, domestic assistance or respite care. While grants can be payable for items of furniture and household equipment, this is mainly for people who are leaving residential care or with a likely risk of entering care. Whether someone receives a payment or not will also depend on whether they are considered to be of sufficiently high priority, such as whether they fall into one of the 'vulnerable' groups.

The current social fund arrangements could be improved by expanding the regulated fund to cover other 'life events' such as setting up a new home, moving from institutional care, and domestic emergencies (as suggested by the Social Security Advisory Committee), as well as having automatic bonuses paid to income support claimants at regular intervals.[52]

Alternatively, a lump-sum payment could be given to the poorest carers, notably those who have received income support as a carer for two years (see also Chapter 9).

Other suggestions made by the House of Commons Social Security Select Committee could indirectly benefit carers; for example, reviewing the balance of grants in the fund's overall budget and the basis for the relative weighting between client groups; and expanding access to interest-free loans.[53]

COUNCIL TAX

People over age 18 may be liable to pay council tax. The amount payable can be reduced in some circumstances, such as by a 25 per cent discount where only one person lives in the property, or a 'disability reduction' (where the home has been substantially adapted to meet the needs of a disabled resident). The Government has already made a start in helping carers by extending the council tax reduction for disabled people and carers living in Band A properties, as part of the National Carers Strategy. But more could be done.

Some groups of people are also 'discounted' for the purposes of calculating council tax. Unpaid carers may also qualify for a discount, provided that:

- they provide care for at least 35 hours a week to the disabled person; *and*
- they live with the person who needs that support; *and*
- the disabled person also receives the highest rate of the disability living allowance care component, or attendance allowance, or analogous benefits; *and*
- the looked-after person must not be the carer's partner or child (under 18).[54]

People who fall outside this definition and so cannot be discounted are co-resident carers providing care to partners and disabled children, or caring for someone on the middle rate of the disability living allowance care component or lower rate of attendance allowance. This group has a higher council tax bill, and lower benefit, than the discounted carers.

Carers of partners or disabled children, and those on the middle rate of the care component of disability living allowance or the higher rate of attendance allowance, should be eligible for the council tax discount available to other carers.

Carers may also incur costs as a result of needing to pay for items or services which health or social care authorities do not provide, or services that people are expected to pay for. This can be considered as an aspect of social exclusion (see Chapter 3 and Chapter 11).

NOTES

1 E Holzhausen and V Pearlman, *Caring on the Breadline*, Carers National Association, 2000
2 This was an analysis of the General Household Survey: S Arber and J Ginn, 'Class and Caring: a forgotten dimension', *Sociology*, Vol 26 No 4, 1992
3 Using the British Household Panel Survey data for 1991-1996: M Hirst and S Hutton, 'Informal Care Over Time', *Benefits* 28, April/May 2000
4 D Madden and I Walker, *Labour Supply, Health and Caring: evidence from the UK*, Dublin, University College, 1999
5 D Gordon et al, *Poverty and Social Exclusion in Britain*, Joseph Rowntree Foundation, 2000
6 A Marsh et al, *Low-Income Families in Britain: work, welfare and social security in 1999*, DSS Research Report 138, Corporate Document Services, 2001

7 London Economics, *The Economics of Informal Care: a report by London Economics for Carers National Association*, 1998

8 M Hirst and S Hutton, 'Informal Care Over Time', *Benefits* 28, April/May 2000

9 See note 7

10 G Parker and D Lawton, *Different Types of Care, Different Types of Carer: evidence from the General Household Survey*, SPRU/The Stationery Office, 1994

11 See note 8

12 See note 1

13 G Mir et al, *Learning Difficulties and Ethnicity*, Department of Health, March 2001

14 R Chamba et al, *On the Edge: minority ethnic families caring for a severely disabled child*, Joseph Rowntree Foundation/The Policy Press, 1999

15 See note 12

16 Carers UK quote

17 Carers UK quote

18 See note 12

19 Carers UK quote

20 See note 12

21 Carers UK quote

22 L Grant, *Disability and Debt*, Joseph Rowntree Foundation, 1995

23 Carers UK quote

24 See note 10

25 See note 12

26 Carers UK quote

27 HM Treasury, *Savings and Assets for All: the modernisation of Britain's tax and benefit system*, Number eight, April 2001

28 Department of Social Security, *Households Below Average Incomes*, 1994/95 to 1999/00, July 2001

29 L Corti, et al, *Caring and Employment*, Employment Department, 1994

30 Estimate from uprating the original figures by the Retail Price Index from 1986–2001; see note 10

31 See note 10

32 Carers UK quote

33 More than 35 hours a week

34 Department of Social Security, *Family Resources Survey*, Great Britain, 1998-99, 2000

35 See note 10

36 See note 8

37 See note 12

38 Carers UK quote

39 Discussed in L Pickard, 'Policy Options for Informal Carers of Elderly People', in *With Respect to Old Age: research vol 3*, report by the Royal Commission on Long-Term Care, Cm 4192-II/3, 1999

40 Particularly for extra-resident carers

41 S Becker and R Silburn, *We're in this Together: conversations with families in caring relationships*, Carers National Association, 1999

42 Pauline in S Becker and R Silburn, *We're in this Together: conversations with families in caring relationships*, Carers National Association, 1999

43 Social Policy Research Unit, *The Financial Needs and Circumstances of Informal Carers: final report*, DHSS 529 4/89, SPRU, 1989

44 M Hirst and S Baldwin, *Unequal Opportunities: growing up disabled*, SPRU, 1994

45 Quoted in G Parker and D Lawton, *Different Types of Care, Different Types of Carer: evidence from the General Household Survey*, SPRU/The Stationery Office, 1994

46 Carers UK

47 J Paterson, *Disability Rights Handbook*, 24th edition, April 1999–April 2000, Disability Alliance, 1999

48 See note 10

49 See note 12

50 Carers UK quote

51 C Ward, *Family Matters: counting families in*, Department of Health, March 2001

52 See F Bennett, *Laying Bare the Lottery: the social fund examined*, CPAG, 1992

53 House of Commons, *The Social Fund*, Social Security Select Committee Report, HC 232, 2001

54 J Zebedee and M Ward, *Guide to Housing Benefit and Council Tax Benefit 1999-2000*, Chartered Institute of Housing/Shelter, 1999

3 Carers and social exclusion

Some six million people are carers in Britain. They are more vulnerable to the problems of social exclusion: they are isolated from the rest of society because their caring duties tie them to their homes and they may face insecurity in old age because their working lives are disrupted. They play a vital role in our society and they deserve recognition for the work they do and better support from the Government.

(Department of Social Security, *Opportunity for All: tackling poverty and social exclusion*, First Annual Report, Cm 4445, 1999)

VULNERABILITY TO EXCLUSION

While many carers do not have the resources with which to participate fully in community life, not all carers could be considered 'socially excluded'.[1] Saul Becker has argued that it can be difficult to see carers as an excluded group when the activities done by carers are based on notions of love and duty, and often carried out privately within the family home. Policy has tended to focus on carers as a 'deserving' rather than excluded group. Yet it is possible to distinguish between 'being excluded' as the outcome of a process of exclusion, and 'vulnerability' to social exclusion, which emphasises the process of exclusion itself. This is not an inevitable consequence of being a carer; rather, a consequence of the attitudes and practices which have shaped services and responses to carers.

One approach suggested by Becker is to consider the factors that can predispose a carer to social exclusion. These elements are highlighted in Table 3.1, grouped according to personal circumstances of the carer, family circumstances, and factors relating to caring.

TABLE 3.1 **Factors indicating vulnerability to social exclusion**

Personal circumstances
- No source of independent income
- Long-term receipt of benefit
- Difficulty managing financially
- Own ill-health or disability
- Health in past year 'not good'
- Working full or part time in low-paid employment
- Age 18 or under
- Minority ethnic origin (especially Pakistani or Bengali origin)

Family circumstances
- Families on means-tested benefits
- Living in households with below average incomes
- Living in areas of multiple disadvantage (eg, high unemployment, poor housing)

Caring
- Living in families with very high costs of disability and/or care
- Caring for someone whose condition carries stigma (eg, HIV/AIDS, mental ill-health, drug abuse)
- Caring full time
- Co-resident caring
- Caring for three years or more in one episode of caring
- Not had a break of two days since started caring
- No help or support from health or social services agencies
- No help or support from family or friends

Source: S Becker, 'Carers and Indicators of Vulnerability to Social Exclusion', *Benefits* 28, April/May 2000

The 2000 Poverty and Social Exclusion Survey, undertaken by the Office for National Statistics and analysed by university researchers, defined social exclusion along the dimensions of poverty, exclusion from social relations, service exclusion, and labour market exclusion.[2] Having dealt with poverty in the last chapter, the three other dimensions in relation to carers will be considered in this chapter.

EXCLUSION FROM SOCIAL RELATIONS

Carers can often feel isolated. For some carers, the exhaustion, combined with regularly interrupted sleep, discourages any attempt at socialising with others.

'Your social life finishes completely…We're very lonely, I think both of us are. Even though people come. Every couple of days there's some-body here.You always see someone, but, yes, very lonely, even though we see people. Basically it's a very lonely existence.'[3]

The Carers UK (previously Carers National Association) *Caring on the Breadline* survey also shows that lack of money can mean that carers cannot participate in family occasions.

'I cannot afford to travel to family celebrations and buy presents to mark such occasions; worse still, I cannot afford to travel to family funerals or to make commemorative donations or to buy flowers.'

Some of the isolation could be mitigated by building on the progress already made in setting up the carers' website. If carers had access to computers they might be able to communicate by email with formal service organisations and other carers in their own time. Carers could be a priority group for free computer technology in the home.

Carers can also be limited by their own poor health.A third of carers spending more than 20 hours a week caring reported having a limiting longstanding illness, and health problems were more common among older carers (over age 45); carers can experience stress-related illnesses, physical injuries and fatigue.[4] Longitudinal data shows that levels of distress increase during the first year of caring and the risk of anxiety and depression rises progressively with the number of hours devoted to caring each week.[5] Such emotional distress does not appear to decline as caring continues. A survey by Southwark Carers of their own members revealed that three-quarters of carers believed that caring had had a negative effect on their health. Of 218 responses:

- 82 per cent were affected by worry or anxiety;
- 56 per cent reported lack of sleep;
- 48 per cent had depression;
- 40 per cent reported back pain; *and*
- 35 per cent had headaches or migraine.

Almost half (48 per cent) said they had no time to look after their health. Furthermore, fewer than a third had told their doctor that those problems were caused by caring.

Carers' health problems are often not well-catered for by primary health services. In one study of carers of people with learning difficulties, nine out of ten health professionals in the south-west of England saw carers' issues as being for social services, rather than a health responsibility[6] (see also Chapter 11).

SERVICE EXCLUSION

The Poverty and Social Exclusion Survey considered social exclusion to be lack of access to basic services, including those in the home (such as power and water supplies) as well as services outside it. Here the emphasis is on the services that carers may need to support them in their caring role (such as from health or social care agencies).

LACK OF SERVICES

Some carers do not receive any formal support. Two analyses of the General Household Survey have revealed that:

- over a third of carers had no one else to help them, and almost half of carers providing assistance for more than 20 hours a week had had no break since they began caring (see below);
- 59 per cent of all carers were looking after someone who did *not* receive regular visits from health, social or voluntary services; this was particularly reported by carers who lived with the disabled person (75 per cent); *and*
- people being cared for by relatives were less likely (than non-relatives) to be receiving any services, especially if living in the same household, and very elderly people were more likely to receive services than those in the younger age groups.[7]

Very often the carers who are most in need are least likely to receive support services. These could be older carers, carers from minority ethnic groups and those caring for people with learning difficulties. Evidence from a study of the impact of the 1995 Carers Act showed that rationing and priority-setting of services could take place at national, local and front-line practitioner level, which meant that eligible carers were often not receiving an assessment, had limited assistance or experienced delays in obtaining support.[8] In some cases carers also excluded themselves, either because they had been told resources were limited, or they felt guilty about receiving services, or were reluctant to identify themselves as 'carers' if they regarded themselves as family members doing their duty.

Some people with learning difficulties have been excluded from services because they are found to be difficult to handle or present challenging behaviour, and there has been concern that families and carers should not be left to cope unaided.[9] An estimated 25 per cent of people with learning difficulties do not come to the attention of statutory services until their carer becomes too old or is unable to cope.[10]

Even when in touch with services, people may be told their needs are not important enough or that the local authority does not have enough resources to help them.

MRS P – MAKING DO

Mrs P is a 65-year-old South Asian woman whose husband had a stroke. She finds it difficult to help him to the toilet and bathe him.

'I contacted the social worker for a commode, but they refused to give that to him. They say he doesn't need it but I think he does. I don't really need anything else apart from the commode. In the night, when he gets up to go to the loo, I have to take him in the wheelchair. We were offered a commode without wheels, but that is no good to him because he can't walk. Social services told us we had to buy one – but the hospital told us to ask social services for one. I have also asked the social worker for a shower to be fitted because I couldn't manage to give him a bath. The social services gave us a chair which fits into the bath, so I manage to give him a bath that way, but we really need a shower. I applied for a shower in July but we've been told we can't have anything at the moment because of a lack of money.'[11]

POOR SERVICES

Research into the perceptions of disabled people and carers about the assessment process found experiences of uncertainty, confusion, marginalisation and exclusion, including some conflict between carers and social workers about level of risk.[12] Social services departments also tended to categorise people as either users or carers, distorting the reality of reciprocal caring situations, and obscuring the needs of carers who are also disabled.

Many disabled people and carers also faced considerable financial difficulties and although some received help from social workers with applying for social security benefits, this was not standard practice. Neither was help with housing. Increasing social isolation experienced by carers – eg, not going on holiday – was rarely discussed by social workers or even referrals made to other organisations.

PAYING FOR SERVICES

A lack of services, or a delay in having an assessment, may result in carers having to buy in services or equipment – not always possible for people on low incomes. Buying in items can add to the additional costs incurred by carers.

> 'I even have to buy incontinence sheets – £8 per week – as the NHS will not provide them.'[13]

Social services can only charge users for community care services. Even where the disabled person pays a charge, this may be paid from the family budget. Often, however, carers are charged for substitute care if they need to leave the disabled person, for example to work (see also Chapter 7). A survey in the mid-1990s (the Warner study) found increases in charging practices and considerable variations in charges paid by carers, with almost a fifth paying for private as well as social services care (see also Chapter 7).[14]

Paying for a service can result in financial hardship or the service being cancelled or refused. A study of the 1995 Carers Act found that three out of 51 carers had cancelled a service because of the cost and others had not taken the option in the first place.[15]

Up to one in four carers in the Warner study experienced hardship as a result of increased charges, with some cancelling the service provided because of the higher charge.[16] Carers having most difficulty in meeting the costs of services were:

- those with a household income below £120 per week (46 per cent);
- carers under 60 (33 per cent); *and*
- carers who were not in employment (29 per cent).

The *Caring on the Breadline* survey also found 59 per cent of carers had used their own income and savings to pay for alternative care.

Most local authorities now charge, frequently by adopting a means test.[17] Some take account of housing expenditure and a minority, disability-related spending. Some also target disability benefits as a source of income. A third of councils charge against the basic income support, which can leave users with incomes below this minimum.

The Carers and Disabled Children Act 2000 enables local authorities to provide services direct to carers, and to charge carers for them. It is for each council to decide if and what to charge; but they must take into account the person's ability to pay.[18] Carers should not be charged for community care services provided to the people they care for, which includes additional services for carers to take a break. People receiving a direct payment under the Act who are parents of a disabled child who is 16 or 17, or receiving income support, income-based jobseeker's allowance or one of the tax credits, are not be expected to make a contribution towards the cost of services.

THE PROPOSED CHARGING REGIME

During early 2001, the Department of Health produced draft guidance on charging. It proposed that local authorities should treat disability-related benefits (like the severe disability premium and the disability living allowance care component) as available income, although charges should not reduce incomes below income support levels.[19] Disability-related spending (such as laundry, diet, heating, purchase of equipment or transport needed for work) should also be taken into account. Charging policies should avoid creating disincentives to work, but a maximum of 55 per cent of net earnings should be taken into account. (The final guidance had not been issued at the time of writing.)

However, many carers have found that the cost of alternative care while at work exceeds the amount they can earn before losing invalid care allowance (ICA). The earnings limit was increased to £72 per week in 2001, and carers can also offset up to half of their net earnings if paying a non-relative to look after the disabled person when the carer is at work (see also Chapter 7).

MRS JONES – ICA AND INCENTIVES TO WORK

As well as caring for her mother, Mrs Jones undertakes paid work for 20 hours a week, earning £100 net. Her mother refuses to be cared for by anyone from social services and so Mrs Jones pays a neighbour £80 per week to care for her mother while she is at work. In the calculation for ICA, Mrs Jones can deduct half of her net earnings (£50) for alternative care although she actually pays £80. Her weekly earnings (£100) minus allowable deductions for care costs (£50) mean she is treated as having earnings of £50 per week for ICA purposes. This means that she would qualify for £41.75 of ICA. Mrs Jones's actual income is thus £100 earnings and £41.75 ICA, a total of £141.75 per week.

According to the draft guidance, 55 per cent of Mrs Jones's income from earnings can be taken into account when assessing income available to pay charges. This equals £55 of her £100 original weekly wage. In addition to this, Mrs Jones's ICA can also be included in the assessment of income. This means that £55 + £41.75 (£96.75) of Mrs Jones's income can be assessed as income available to pay charges. This amounts to 68 per cent of Mrs Jones's income. Furthermore, no allowance is made for the extra £30 per week alternative care costs not taken into account as part of the ICA calculation.[20]

Unlike earnings, the draft guidance proposes that all of a pension income can be taken into account.

GERALD DAVIES – PAYING 100 PER CENT OF HIS PENSION FOR CARE

Gerald Davies is 45 years old and cares full time for his mother, who has Alzheimer's disease. His income consists of a small occupational pension and ICA, and he has a small amount of savings. Mr Davies has a low income, but it is just above the income support level. He considers that his occupational pension provides an income, and his ICA provides recognition of his caring role. If Mr Davies receives any services to help him in his caring role, the local authority could include all of his ICA and his occupational pension in the calculation of his income available to be assessed to pay charges.

PARTNER PAYS

Local authorities vary as to whether partners or spouses are asked about their income and capital and whether this is included in the calculation of what someone has to pay. The Warner study referred to above also showed that carers often contribute towards the disabled person's charge:

- In almost two-thirds of cases, the carer's income was used to pay the charge.
- In 28 per cent of cases the joint income of the disabled person and carer was used to pay the charge. [21]

Often, carers appeared to be paying for services when there was no legal obligation to do so, which may have reflected the low income in households containing a disabled person and a carer. A recent Ombudsman's investigation found that a council's inclusion of a spouse's ICA and carer premium in the initial assessment was wrong; however, it could take into account a spouse's means in deciding whether to reduce the charge on hardship grounds.[22] Carers UK has also found that some local authorities have charged disabled people at the highest rate if their spouse carer refuses to provide details of their finances.[23] There is also a danger that the cumulative effect of charging a disabled person and a carer could plunge some families into financial hardship.

MR O'CONNER – PAYING FOR SERVICES TO HIS WIFE

Janet O'Conner cares for her next door neighbour, who is frail and has severe arthritis. Janet receives ICA, and from April 2001, under the Carers and Disabled Children Act 2000, her local authority can now provide services to help her to care and charge her for these. Mr O'Conner, Janet's husband, is in paid employment. As the proposals stand, Mr O'Conner's income could be assessed as income available to pay charges for his wife's caring-related services.

The new charging regime should exempt ICA as well as the carer premium from charging; carers on income support should not be charged; spending on alternative care should be considered as part of disability-related expenses and so disregarded; savings should be ignored, and only income from capital taken into account (as proposed for the pension credit).

GETTING A BREAK – RESPITE CARE AND PAYING FOR IT

Carers in the *Caring on the Breadline* survey reported that they frequently could not get a break from caring.[24] For some it is a question of getting appropriate care; for others, it is the cost. In some cases, the cared-for person did not want care from anyone else (perhaps reflecting some of the tensions described in Chapter 2), so the carers did not get a break. Among those caring for more than 20 hours a week, 49 per cent had not had a break of at least two days since starting caring.[25] Mencap estimates that only 40 per cent of family carers of people with learning disabilities have a break.[26]

The Government is committed to giving 75,000 more carers some respite,[27] but the evidence suggests that to date, many councils have failed to meet their target. The Carers Special Grant was intended to enable social services departments to develop short-term break services, which were more flexible and diverse to fit around carers' needs, rather than carers having to fit in with existing service provision. A study by Carers UK of the impact of the first year of the Grant (1999/2000) in the north of England found that just over half of the local authorities had not used it directly for breaks.[28] Other research also found that about a third of councils had spent less than their 75 per cent target; furthermore, only 2 per cent of the total Grant had been spent on services for minority ethnic carers.[29]

A carer may be able to keep ICA during the period of a break; but may have to pay for any services used during this time. ICA rules allow a break of up to 12 weeks within a 26-week period, of which four weeks can be for a temporary break, like having a holiday or the cared-for person receiving alternative (respite) care. Carers can be paid ICA for any week in which they are caring for at least 35 hours so odd days or weekends away are unlikely to affect entitlement.[30]

In one case, the cost of a fortnight's break was £600, so it is not surprising that many carers find paying for respite difficult.

'Nursing home fees for respite care every five weeks are a constant strain.'

'I cannot get a carer to relieve me as the pay is so low for the responsibility involved. No one will do it for £6 an hour. I have been asking social services for two years now.'[31]

VOUCHERS FOR BREAKS

The Carers and Disabled Children Act will allow local authorities to give vouchers when a carer needs a break, to cover services that the carer would otherwise have provided. Detailed regulations are expected to be laid in October 2001 or later.

Some local authorities have introduced voucher schemes in advance of the regulations. However, research commissioned by Carers UK found that carers had little experience of vouchers: most of the carers used family, friends and neighbours for alternative care (34 per cent), followed by social services cover (17 per cent) and day centres (13 per

cent). One in ten had no alternative care arrangements. Carers believe that vouchers should:

- involve the screening of paid workers, continuity of and appropriate paid care;
- offer the care worker of their, or the disabled person's, choice;
- not affect their income and benefits;
- have a long life-span and not be mean-tested.[32]

A small sample of employers felt that they should also be able to top up vouchers, but that vouchers should be exempt from national insurance contributions.

Carers suggest that vouchers for breaks could be made as a direct payment; could also include a regular, weekly day off; cover more than two weeks' respite; and go to the carer in some cases.

EMPLOYMENT EXCLUSION

It has been estimated that some 13 per cent of all people in paid employment have some caring responsibility.[33] However, employers are not always flexible in their approach to people with caring responsibilities:

- In one Carers UK report, 83 per cent of carers in a paid job said that their employer knew about their caring responsibilities, but 29 per cent said their employer was unhelpful.[34]
- Some participants in the New Deal 50plus had caring responsibilities, and felt that employers were not particularly sympathetic to them.[35] One instance was quoted of a man who was called to London to look after his mother the day he was due to start work, but despite informing the company, someone else had filled the vacancy before he returned.

Given the propensity for poorer people to become full-time carers (see Chapter 2), there may also be a labour market effect. For instance, there seems to be regional variations in the proportion of carers who are working. Only about 30 per cent of the 35,000 carers in Wales are currently in employment – a much lower figure than in England (see also Chapter 4).[36]

Some carers may be unable to work at all because their caring responsibilities take up so much time or mean that they cannot commit themselves to regular hours.[37]

Parent carers may encounter particular difficulties with getting and staying in paid employment.

WHAT PREVENTS PARENT CARERS FROM WORKING?

Parents of a disabled child are less likely to work than other parents; only two out of ten mothers with a disabled child are working, compared with six out of ten mothers overall.[38] However, there is evidence of a desire to be in paid work: 29 per cent of mothers with one disabled child and 50 per cent of those with two disabled children would prefer to be in paid employment than at home.[39] The combined impact of the limited availability of flexible work locally, and the lack of suitable and affordable childcare, can effectively rule out working for parents looking after a disabled child; work has to be compatible with the demands of caring.[40] One parent carer whose child became ill unpredictably in about one week in four told Carers UK that, in order to work, she needed:

> 'guaranteed cover if my child were ill so I could think of getting a job without letting people down.'

There is also an assumption that mothers of disabled children do not work, and so are available to deal with professionals at any time.[41]

There are an estimated 380,000 disabled children and young people (to age 17) in Britain, and an estimated 308,000 fathers and 76,000 mothers of disabled children are in full- or part-time work.[42] Parents of disabled children who are in work are more likely to need time off for hospital appointments or at key points during a child's life, and the need for time off is likely to remain during childhood. Grandparents may be less prepared to help out when children get older, especially as they themselves get more frail.

FLEXIBLE EMPLOYMENT

The National Carers Strategy included a number of suggestions to make employment more 'carer-friendly'. The Government has made some progress in extending the rights of employees to time off, primarily for working parents, but also including time off in emergencies for employees who also have some caring responsibilities for other people (but only two or three days). Many employees with caring responsibilities can resolve short-term care problems if given the flexibility to reorganise

their working time; people are more confident of doing so if offered a limited number of paid or unpaid days special leave for emergencies or special circumstances.[43] Arrangements that recognise domestic responsibilities legitimately are preferable to having to take 'sick' days. From the employers' perspective, more flexible employment patterns which recognise caring responsibilities can result in reduced sickness absence and improved retention, recruitment, productivity and morale of staff.[44]

However, the evidence points to difficulties in combining paid work and caring. Caring can have a detrimental effect on the carer's work (eg, low productivity, absences and having to leave early). A study of employers by Hilary Arksey revealed concern on the part of some employers that giving special treatment to carers might create resentment on the part of other workers.[45] While men are increasingly becoming carers, male-dominated workplaces have been less likely to offer flexible arrangements for caring. There is evidence that informal arrangements (such as shift-swapping) can help carers as much as formal arrangements for leave and supportive line managers. However, Arksey concludes that support for working carers entails a greater input from services as much as more flexibility from employers (see below and also Chapter 11).

TIME OFF FOR WORKING CARERS

Since December 1999, parents of disabled children have had the right to take 13 weeks' leave at any point up to the child's 18th birthday, which can be in blocks of time of less than a week; this is to be extended to a total of 18 weeks.[46] An estimated 77,000 fathers and 38,000 mothers are expected to take up the additional five weeks' leave entitlement. Time off can also include cases where the employee needs to make longer-term care arrangements for someone who falls ill or is injured, and can include someone who relies on the employee for assistance (such as someone for whom the employee cares after work, or an elderly neighbour).

MAKING WORK PAY

The provision for time off does not include a right to pay, which is left to employer's discretion. There could be a significant minority of people who would lose pay if taking time off; a Department of Trade and Industry survey found that although nearly half of employees would be able to take paid leave when taking time off in an emergency, 19 per cent said they would take unpaid leave and 15 per cent said they would make up time later.[47]

The Government has estimated that, in most cases, emergencies would be dealt with in one or two days, although there is no limit as to the frequency that an employee can exercise this right. The provision is intended to cover emergencies which are unforeseen, and so other provisions (such as parental leave) would be more appropriate for more regular or longer absences. However, it may be that in some cases time off is required to meet the unpredictable needs of a cared-for person (such as someone in mental distress who needs attention intermittently). In such cases it might be that if leave is unpaid the person incurs significant financial loss. If so, perhaps consideration could be given to a route into the proposed employment tax credit (see Chapter 10) on an emergency basis.

Some carers and parents may be less skilled or qualified, and so may think it is not worthwhile financially to work – either because the wages would be low, or if a tenant, that they might lose housing benefit. There may also be additional costs involved when working (such as higher travel costs or alternative care) which may limit the financial incentive to enter paid employment. One parent carer told Carers UK:

> 'Because I pay a childminder at double the price (because my child has special needs) I find at the end of the month I really do not have any money left.'[48]

The Government has extended eligibility for the childcare tax credit to cover approved childcare, and up to age 16 for disabled children.[49] In addition, since October 2000, the working families' tax credit has included a disabled child's premium. The Carers and Disabled Children Act also allows direct payments (in lieu of community care services) to parent carers.

While these changes should help parent carers to be better off financially in work, other carers may need additional support (such as through an enhanced tax credit – see Chapter 10).

RETENTION

Hitherto, the overall policy emphasis has assumed that caring responsibilities are the preserve of younger women with children, rather than older women (and men) who provide care for adults.[50] However, the Institute for Public Policy Research has recently suggested that 'work-life balance' issues could apply to carers across the lifecycle and so include other carers.[51]

Having the flexibility to take time off to deal with emergencies could be more valuable than fixed periods of leave or 'career breaks' (which may be more appropriate for women with children). The pattern of caring responsibilities reflects the needs of the cared-for person, and so in some cases (such as when caring for someone with mental distress) may be cyclical or unpredictable. As intensity of care may increase and duration is unknown, it may be more appropriate to be supported within employment than to have to take a break from it. Evidence from the British Household Panel Survey suggests that the longer the time spent caring, the less likely it becomes that carers will be in paid work compared with non-carers; after the third year, those providing care for more than 20 hours a week are considerably less likely to be in paid work.[52]

A strategy to help retain employees who have some caring responsibilities could be of particular benefit to women; other research has noted that, in the year of starting co-resident caring, women were more likely to be in employment and less likely to be inactive than in the previous year.[53] This suggests that, while extra-resident care can be combined with paid employment, co-resident care may be more difficult to do so. In some cases, people might be able to stay in paid employment longer when their caring responsibilities start, if offered more flexibility and time off by employers.

If unpaid, breaks could be financially supported through an extension to the employment tax credit (see Chapter 10). Self-employed people may also need some financial 'buffer' if taking some time off for caring.

Flexible employment practices, perhaps in conjunction with an extension to the employment tax credit, might help working carers to retain paid employment for longer.

PROGRESSION

The new emphasis on employment sustainability, which was being considered by the Department for Education and Employment (now the Department for Work and Pensions) in relation to the New Deal for young people, could be adapted to the needs of carers. Caring responsibilities can be a potential barrier to career development and progression, so carers may need early advice on how to combine work and caring. This role could perhaps be fulfilled by a variety of agencies, using the personal adviser model. However, at this important early stage if a carer is not likely to be claiming benefit then s/he will have no cause to go to the Jobcentre Plus service. Either a 'progression' service needs to be developed within Jobcentre Plus, or located elsewhere, for instance linked to voluntary sector and employer advice networks, or even as part of the renewal process for tax credits (see also Chapter 10 on the role of tax credits in retention). As part of a 'seamless' progression service, better out-of-hours help from health and social care agencies needs to be available for working carers who cannot contact those agencies within 'normal' working hours.

Carers in contact with the Jobcentre Plus could continue to have access to a specialist personal adviser during the first six or twelve months back in work after a period spent caring.

A 'progression' service could be developed within Jobcentre Plus, voluntary sector and employer networks, or could be linked to the renewal process for tax credits.

Better out-of-hours services for health and support are also needed for working carers.

Payments for care which offer an incentive to care can encourage the combination of work and care, and could improve the take-up of part-time work or self-employment.[54] This suggests that the options discussed above to improve ICA, income support and tax credits for carers who are presently out of the labour market could also have a positive effect on the take-up of part-time work.

NOTES

1   S Becker, 'Carers and Indicators of Vulnerability to Social Exclusion', *Benefits* 28, April/May 2000
2   D Gordon et al, *Poverty and Social Exclusion in Britain*, Joseph Rowntree Foundation, 2000
3   Peggy, a working-age carer, in S Becker and R Silburn, *We're in this Together: conversations with families in caring relationships*, Carers National Association, 1999
4   See for example, M Hirst and H Arksey, 'Informal Carers Count', *Nursing Standard*, Vol 14, No 42, 33-24, 2000; and O Rowlands and G Parker, *Informal Carers: results of an independent study carried out on behalf of the Department of Health as part of the 1995 General Household Survey*, National Statistics, 1998
5   M Hirst, 'Trends in Informal Care in Great Britain During the 1990s',

Health and Social Care in the Community, 9, 2001

6 V Williams and C Robinson, *A Seamless Service: the interface between social services and health and what it means for carers of people with learning disabilities in the South West of England*, SPRU, 1998

7 O Rowlands and G Parker, *Informal Carers: results of an independent study carried out on behalf of the Department of Health as part of the 1995 General Household Survey*, National Statistics, 1998; and G Parker and D Lawton, *Different Types of Care, Different Types of Carer: evidence from the General Household Survey*, SPRU/The Stationery Office, 1994

8 H Arksey et al, *Carers Needs and the Carers Act: an evaluation of process and outcomes of assessment*, SPRU, 2000

9 Department of Health, *Valuing People: a new strategy for learning disability for the 21st Century*, Cm 5086, March 2001

10 See note 9

11 A Davis et al, *Access to Assessment: perspectives of practitioners, disabled people and carers*, Joseph Rowntree Foundation/Community Care, 1997

12 See note 11

13 Carers UK quote

14 N Warner, *Better Tomorrows: report of a national study of carers and community care charges*, 1995

15 See note 8

16 See note 14

17 Audit Commission, *Charging with Care: how councils charge for home care*, 2000

18 Department of Health, *Carers and People with Parental Responsibility for Disabled Children: policy guidance*, 2001

19 Department of Health, *Fairer Charging Policies for Home Care and Other Non-residential Services: a consultation paper*, January 2001

20 Examples in this section from Carers UK's response to the consultation on the draft Guidance, *Fairer Charging Policies for Home Care and other Non-residential Social Services*, March 2001.

21 See note 14

22 Quoted in G Tait et al, *Paying for Care Handbook*, 2nd edition, CPAG, 2001

23 See note 20

24 E Holzhausen and V Pearlman, *Caring on the Breadline: the financial implications of caring*, Carers National Association, 2000

25 O Rowlands and G Parker, *Informal Carers: results of an independent study carried out on behalf of the Department of Health as part of the 1995 General Household Survey*, National Statistics, 1998

26 Quoted in C Ward, *Family Matters: counting families in*, Department of Health, March 2001

27 Department of Health, *The NHS Plan: a plan for investment, a plan for reform*, Cm 4818-I, July 2000

28 Carers National Association, *Give Us a Break: a study of the impact of the Carers Special Grant in the North of England*, Carers National Association, 2000

29 P Banks and E Roberts, *More Breaks for Carers? An analysis of local authority plans*

and progress reports on the use of the Carers Special Grant (Year 2), Kings Fund, 2001

30 See note 22

31 Carers UK quote

32 L Daniels and L McCarraher, *Research into Vouchers to Provide Breaks for Carers*, Carers National Association, 2001

33 Work–Life Balance Baseline Survey: summary, November 2000

34 Carers National Association, *The True Cost of Caring: a survey of carers' lost income*, CNA, 1996

35 J Kodz and J Eccles, *Evaluation of New Deal 50plus: Qualitative Evidence from Clients: second phase*, Employment Service Research and Development Report ESR70, March 2001

36 Department for Education and Employment, *Changing Patterns in a Changing World*, 2000

37 A Stephenson, *Work and Welfare: attitudes, experiences and behaviour – nineteen low-income families*, DSS In-house Report 76, July 2001

38 Parents at Work, *Altering The Balance: overcoming barriers to work for parents of disabled children, 1997*

39 D Lawton, *Complex Numbers: families with more than one disabled child*, SPRU, 1998

40 C Kagan et al, *Caring to Work: accounts of working parents of disabled children*, Family Policy Studies Centre, 1998

41 See note 40

42 Department of Trade and Industry regulatory impact statement, based on OPCS estimates

43 S Bevan et al, F*amily-Friendly Employment: the business case*, DfEE Research Report 136, 1999

44 See note 43

45 H Arskey, *Employers' Provisions for Carers*, SPRU, March 2001

46 See note 42

47 In workplaces with more than 25 staff: M Cully et al, *Britain at Work: as depicted by the 1998 Workplace Employee Relations Survey*, Routledge, 1999

48 Carers UK quote

49 Inland Revenue Press Release, 13 May 1999

50 See for example, L Pickard, 'Policy Options for Informal Carers of Elderly People', in *With Respect to Old Age: research vol 3*, report by the Royal Commission on Long–Term Care, Cm 4192–II/3, 1999

51 L Harker and S Lewis, 'Work–Life Policies: where should the government go next? in N Burkitt (ed), *A Life's Work: full and fulfilling employment*, Institute for Public Policy Research, 2001

52 M Hirst 'Trends in Informal Care in Great Britain during the 1990s', *Health and Social Care in the Community*, 2001

53 London Economics, *The Economics of Informal Care: a report by London Economics for Carers National Association*, 1998

54 See for example, C Glendinning and E McLaughlin, *Paying for Care: lessons from Europe*, Social Security Advisory Commitee Research Report 5, HMSO, 1993

4 Caring and transitions

As we saw in Chapter 1, while some carers spend considerable periods of time providing care, there are many who only care for short periods; more than a third of carers start or end care-giving each year.[1] In one study, two-thirds of co-resident carers were not caring five years earlier, and three-quarters of those caring for more than 20 hours a week were not doing so five years earlier.

Many individuals can expect to provide care during some period of their lives; the British Household Panel Survey data suggests that by the age of 75, almost two-thirds of women and close to half of men will have provided one or more spells of at least 20 hours of care per week.[2]

For some carers, such as those caring for disabled children or adults with learning difficulties, caring is likely to be a lifelong commitment, and such carers have to cope and adjust to a number of different challenges in transitions in their caring career. For instance, a carer of a child with a learning difficulty (sometimes referred to as having 'special needs') has to adjust to:

- being told their child has a learning difficulty;
- making choices about education when the child reaches school age;
- adolescence and the move to adult services;
- the son or daughter leaving home – in adulthood;
- growing older together;
- when illness or bereavement makes it difficult to care.[3]

Many family carers of people with learning difficulties are also caring for more than one person (perhaps ageing parents or grandchildren).[4] For others, such as those caring for adults with severe mental distress, caring can be sporadic or cyclical. The carer may not be physically or practically caring at all at certain times, but still be anxious and stressed waiting for, or trying to prevent, a crisis. Similarly, people caring for someone with a progressive condition might have a fluctuating pattern of care-giving.

People who spend shorter periods caring may be less likely to encounter poverty and social exclusion (see Chapter 3), but a period of caring can affect future income and hardship for former carers (see below). In order to tackle the poverty and exclusion faced by carers, consideration needs to be given to transitions in and out of caring as much as to the 'status' of being a carer.

This chapter examines some of the evidence on the movement into and out of caring, as well as those who stay caring, and some of the processes which might be involved.

CONCEPTS OF TRANSITIONS AND TRAJECTORIES

In recent years, the emergence of longitudinal research (such as the British Household Panel Survey data), following people over time has challenged some of the assumptions based on a 'snapshot' of a particular group of people at a single moment. 'Transitions' and 'trajectories' are key concepts in the associated 'dynamic' approach social policy, and are intended to help us understand how time can affect different groups of people.[5] This adds the dimension of time' (duration on benefit or in poverty), so the focus can move to 'spells' in a particular state (such as poverty) rather than simply characteristics of the people involved. Individuals are conceptualised as following trajectories, comprising a sequence of states and transitions, but not necessarily always in a fixed or linear way. Trajectories can occur in different domains of life (eg, in the family or in employment) and trajectories within these different domains may intersect, such as where family breakdown has an impact on employment prospects.

Associated with this use of panel data, another research method uses individual case studies (the 'biographical' approach) to understand how people make sense of their lives. A study comparing carers in Britain and Germany described how carers understood the processes and role changes involved in being a carer.[6] While caring may arise as a contingency, as it develops it becomes a process within which carers need to adjust perspectives of their own lives to accommodate caring into their own experiences. Some carers may understand their role as a continuation of a their family responsibilities; some may take on caring as a new identity (perhaps getting involved with campaigning groups); others may have made 'reluctant transitions', stemming from a personal crisis, often involving a painful reorientation. Over time, carers involved in that research had undergone processes of change and adapted not only to changing circumstances but to the changing needs of the cared-for person. For some carers, accepting formal help and residential care was part of a slow process of moving away from family-based care into co-operation with more formal provision.

TRANSITIONS IN AND OUT OF CARING

People who provide care do not always identify themselves as 'carers', as they are doing 'what is necessary' for a loved one. Some decisions to care are precipitated by illness or crisis, and are taken with little time to consider the implications.[7]

London Economics carried out an analysis of the British Household Panel Survey for Carers UK (previously Carers National Association), focussing on 'caring transitions', and this section draws heavily on that study.[8] However, it has limitations as it only covers five years of the Survey, and emphasises the characteristics of carers rather than *spells of caring*, so we are unable to detect any patterns of caring *trajectories*.[9] Further research is needed into 'spells' of caring and what factors affect them – for instance, does having several short spells of caring subsequently lead to a longer spell? Or are there quite different patterns of caring involved? Some people are also caring for more than one person (perhaps in particular, carers from minority ethnic communities – see Chapter 1).

Karen, interviewed by Deardon and Becker, has provided care for several relatives over several years, and has never entered the labour market:

KAREN

Karen is 22 and lives with her parents and older brother. Her grandparents live close by. Karen's mother has been ill since Karen was 12 and initially Karen took on domestic tasks, helped by her grandmother, and personal care, such as helping her mother to wash. When Karen was 16 her grandmother had a severe stroke and Karen took on the role of providing care for her as well. She receives invalid care allowance and is classed as her mother's full-time carer, although she is also providing a high level of practical and personal support to her grandmother and emotional support to her grandfather.

Further research into spells of caring, and having a better understanding of 'caring transitions', would also enable us to deepen our understanding of the processes involved in social exclusion (as highlighted in Chapter 3).

STOPPING AND STARTING

There is a surprising amount of stopping and starting of caring. The available information shows that 40 per cent of carers stop and start in any single year, and that there is a higher turnover of people who provide extra-resident care.

A longer period of panel data (from 1991 to 1998) indicates a decline in the proportion of extra-resident carers and an expansion in co-resident carers and in those providing more substantial amounts of care.[10]

Given the differences between co-resident and extra-resident care, the two will be considered separately. The following section is drawn from regression analysis of the British Household Panel Survey carried out by London Economics for Carers UK.

PROPENSITY TO START CO-RESIDENT CARE

People are more likely to start to care for someone in their own household if:

- they were a co-resident carer in the previous year;
- they live in a household with less than five people;
- the cared-for individual receives disability benefits;
- they live in Wales (perhaps reflecting poorer health and an ageing population);
- they are in rented accommodation.

Conversely, they are *less* likely to be a co-resident carer if they have higher qualifications, were employed in the previous year or have higher household income. Age and gender do not appear to have as much significance in this analysis.

PROPENSITY TO START EXTRA-RESIDENT CARE

People are more likely to start to care for someone outside of the household if:

- they were an extra-resident carer in the previous year;
- they belong to an organisation/group;
- they have an active religious affiliation;
- their highest qualification was at A/O level;
- they have higher investment income;
- they are female;
- they live in Wales;
- they live in the Midlands;
- they made more visits to their GP in the previous year;
- they have use of a car.

Conversely they are less likely to be an extra-resident carer if they have greater wealth, were previously in full-time employment, have young children and do not own a car. The last two characteristics may reflect the opportunity costs of *time*, whereas the propensity to start co-resident care seems to be more likely to reflect the opportunity costs of *income* – eg, qualifications and employment.

The national unemployment rate seems to have little impact on the propensity to provide care, but a *higher level of unemployment seems to increase the number of hours spent caring for someone in another household* – the higher the unemployment, the longer the hours. This might reflect the greater difficulty in finding a job as a time of high unemployment, as well as the limited time available for jobsearch, and the types of work available (see also Chapter 1). Some of the characteristics affecting the *numbers of hours of care* provided are listed in Table 4.1.

While many people spent a long period caring (see below), both policy and practice need to reflect the transitions into and out of caring. Given the high turnover of carers, there needs to be provision for better transitions into and out of caring, which reduce the likelihood that carers and ex-carers fall into social exclusion, as well as maintaining and supporting carers in their role.

TRANSITIONS INTO CARING

Public services could be more alert to situations where people begin to take on a caring role, and offer appropriate support. For example, social

TABLE 4.1: **Relative importance of various characteristics on hours of care**

	Co-resident (average 41 hrs)	Extra-resident (average 9 hrs)
Male	–	-0.8
Full-time work last period	10.7	–
Lives in Wales	+17.8	+2.1
Single	- 15.0	–
National unemployment rate	–	+0.8 per percentage point
Cared-for receives attendance allowance	+13.3	–
Rented accommodation	–	+1.9

Source: London Economics, *The Economics of Informal Care: a report by London Economics for Carers National Association*, 1998

care services need to focus on the whole family, and the needs of disabled parents, to help young carers and prevent them from taking on inappropriate caring roles. Similarly, health services could also ensure that adequate support and information is made available (eg, at hospital ward and primary care trust level) to people who might take on a caring role for a patient after a period in acute care.

Research evidence, including studies commissioned by the former Department of Social Security (DSS) (now the Department for Work and Pensions) suggests that many people become aware of benefits like invalid care allowance (ICA) some time *after* they begin caring.[11] Carers may be missing out on basic entitlement, as well as being affected by rules which limit the backdating of benefit.[12]

Carers may be under severe time pressure and may also be unable to leave the cared-for person except by arrangement, having little and incomplete information about benefits.[13] There is often little understanding of the distinction between the benefits that a carer and the disabled person are entitled to. There is also limited awareness of ICA *per se* and the carer premium. Almost half of carers in one Carers UK survey were not receiving ICA even though the majority of these (89 per cent) had been caring for more than 35 hours a week.[14] The label 'carer' may be seen as acceptable and appropriate but this was not so easy for 'family carers' – ie, those looking after a spouse or elderly relatives.[15] This is seen as the usual family relationship, so it may rarely occur to people to make a claim.

People who are beginning to take on a caring role need immediate, high-quality information about benefits and services. This needs to be available from a variety of public services, from Jobcentre Plus, through to social services, health centres and hospitals.

More 'carer-friendly' employment could focus on helping carers when they are in a job, rather than waiting until they have given up work (see Chapter 3).

TRANSITIONS OUT OF CARING

Although many carers, notably parents of a disabled child, will be caring for long periods, others may only be doing so for a relatively short time. Early planning and assistance with the steps towards a new role may be needed.

People may leave a caring role for a variety of reasons. This could include situations where parent carers are preparing their children for independent living. Young people aged 16 and 17 may want to have control of their own support, such as receiving a direct payment in lieu of community care services, which is now available to young disabled people under new legislation. This transition can be recognised through social services and transition planning for the young disabled person through new Connexions service. Other situations include where a disabled or elderly person might enter residential care (perhaps for a long or short-term placement).

In both circumstances, carers may need support if they are to relinquish or reduce their role.

Agencies in contact with carers could also help them build and maintain human and social capital during a period of caring – this could help someone to prepare for the time when caring ceases (discussed in Chapter 7).

BEREAVEMENT

Caring may cease dramatically upon the death of the cared-for person, requiring the carer to make a rapid transition into another role. The benefits system has offered little breathing space to carers in this position, as although the carer premium can run on for eight weeks after caring ceases, ICA stops immediately. The short-term financial impact can be dramatic; for instance in one case, a two-parent family with a working father lost 25 per cent of their net monthly income when their child died as child benefit, disability living allowance and ICA entitlement were all lost.[16]

The Government has announced that ICA will be extended for eight weeks after the death of the cared-for person. This should benefit some 10,000–15,000 carers every year.[17] The eight-week run-on of the carer premium and proposed extension to ICA for the same period should give ex-carers some breathing space before having to be available for work, when people become redefined from 'carers' to 'jobseekers'. It should also protect the carer's national insurance contribution record.

Better phasing-out of other benefits was also suggested in a study considering the financial impact on parents when their child dies; for instance, disability living allowance could 'run-on' for three months (the same length of time as the waiting period).[18]

The same study also noted that survivors' benefits also tend to be associated with the death of a breadwinner, rather than a child. Funeral payments could also be increased to reflect the costs of a funeral, as recommended by the House of Commons Social Security Select Committee.[19]

Some parents in the study received standardised Benefits Agency letters when their child died, referring to the 'deceased', and over-payments were not always explained; this was often experienced as 'cold' and 'hurtful', and contrasted with situations where a kind letter was sent acknowledging the return of an order book or a sympathetic phone call was made.[20] Similarly, an evaluation of the ONE service (described in Chapter 7) found that the personal adviser service was valued by those who had recently lost a partner (through death or separation) and allowed them the space and sympathy to come to terms with their new situation.[21]

When a death has been notified, a former carer could be signposted to bereavement counselling (optional) and other support services, as well as being offered work-focussed help.

Carers may need support when their caring activity ceases, such as when a young disabled person leaves home or the cared-for person dies. This can include using transition planning for young

people through the Connexions service, or using the process of notifying a death as a trigger to signpost carers for potential support. Agencies should review their procedures when someone dies to ensure that contact with relatives and carers is routinely undertaken with sensitivity.

SUPPORTING CARING

Over the past two decades, carers have become increasingly recognised for making an important contribution to society and as a group 'deserving' of support. Eighty-two per cent of the public (across all political preferences) believe that more should be spent on carers (the group seen as most 'deserving').[22] Other research has shown that both individuals and employers believed that the Government should contribute to pensions for carers.[23]

People who have been caring for long periods are among those most at risk of poverty and social exclusion.[24] The *Caring on the Breadline* survey of carers revealed that the longer the time spent caring, the greater the financial difficulties encountered.[25] People may have been caring for some time before claiming ICA, or being assessed for social services help.[26]

The London Economics analysis also highlighted characteristics of the people who are more likely to stay caring. These are:

- Co-resident carers who have received ICA.
- Co-resident carers looking after individuals with severe health problems/recipients of disability living allowance/attendance allowance.
- Those who have spent a longer time caring.
- Those who spend more hours caring (if they are co-resident carers).

Cash support can be one way of maintaining care. An international study for the Social Security Advisory Committee suggested that, on the whole, cash payments did not seem to influence the choice to *begin* caring and have not resulted in lowering the overall rates of residential care.[27] However, payments can help *sustain* caring for longer than would otherwise be the case, helping support carers in their role even if the overall supply of carers is not increased.

Benefits like ICA, therefore, can play an important role in helping carers continue to provide care. This highlights the importance of benefits, concessions and services (Chapters 2, 9 and 10) which can help support carers.

One key objective for benefits and services for carers is to support them in their role, in particular focussing improvements on those who may be caring for extended periods of time.

FORMER CARERS

Even if someone stops caring, it is likely that a spell of care will have had an effect on financial and employment prospects. A study for the DSS found that the incomes of ex-carers tended to be substantially below average.[28]

One comparison of people who were not caring in the first year with those who completed a spell of caring, found that former carers (particularly those caring for someone in the same household) had lower incomes in the year after caring ceased than those who had not taken up caring.[29] Female carers had lower incomes in the year after caring finished (£770 for those formerly co-resident and £250 for former extra-resident carers), whereas formerly co-resident men had incomes £1,300 lower.[30] Women were less likely to be in full-time employment in the years after being a co-resident carer; this picture is reversed for extra-resident carers. Male co-resident carers were shown to lose £26 a week and female extra-resident carers £5 a week.

Carers who have provided substantial amounts of care are less likely to be in paid work when a period of care-giving ends; not only do they take longer to return to work but the number in paid work continues to decline after caring has ceased. Over six waves of the British Household Panel Survey there seems to be little evidence that the incomes of former carers catch up after finishing care, especially after longer and more recent periods of caring.[31]

People who have an interrupted work record because of caring are likely to have lower pension entitlement (see Chapter 8), and some who cease caring over the age of 40 have found it difficult to return to work, and have had particularly low employment rates after they ceased caring.[32]

Caring on the Breadline found that the concerns of former carers differed slightly from current carers; almost seven out of ten former carers said they were worse off since becoming carers and still had problems, such as paying utility bills and paying for essential repairs.[33] One in five former carers also had to cut back on buying food. Financial problems appear to persist long after caring has ceased.

'Since my mother died, income is less, expenses similar and job prospects poor due to my age.'[34]

Former carers are less likely to believe that they will be worse off in the future (44 per cent) compared with current carers (61 per cent), which may reflect the fact that former carers are more likely to be older, some over pension age – 69 per cent of former carers are over age 60. Former carers are more likely to be receiving bereavement allowance (and so may have been caring for a husband or wife who has subsequently died).[35]

> [Financial situation] 'worse since I stopped being a carer because I am now on a pension and can get no benefits myself.'

People may also have support needs relating to their former role as a carer. The Southwark Carers survey found that quarter of former carers still used its services. The Scottish Executive has suggested that someone could continue to be regarded as a carer after caring ends, perhaps for a period of eight weeks, and so continue to receive support services.[36] People may need support with their own emotional and health needs as well as managing new financial circumstances.

Former carers can encounter financial difficulties following a period of caring, even some time after caring has ceased. The new agencies (Jobcentre Plus and the Pensions Service) can help carers to develop human and social capital during a period of caring, which they can later use when caring has ceased. In particular, agencies need to be more proactive in identifying and assisting former carers. They may have ongoing financial, health and support needs, and so services need to ensure that former carers receive support in their own right during this period of transition.

Carers are not an homogenous group – so the next four chapters focus on some of the aspects facing specific types of carers; those with caring responsibilities at a relatively young age (Chapter 5), parent carers looking after their disabled children (Chapter 6), carers of working age (Chapter 7) and finally older carers (Chapter 8).

NOTES

1 Social Policy Research Unit, 'Informal Carers: a moving target', *Cash and Care*, Winter 1999

2 M Hirst 'Trends in Informal Care in Great Britain during the 1990s', *Health and Social Care in the Community,* 9, 2001

3 C Ward, *Family Matters: counting families in*, Department of Health, March 2001

4 See note 3

5 L Leisering and R Walker (eds), *The Dynamics of Modern Society: poverty policy and welfare*, The Policy Press, 1998

6 P Chamberlayne and A King, *Cultures of Care: biographies of carers in Britain and the two Germanies*, The Policy Press, 2000

7 J Healy and S Yarrow, *Family Matters: parents living with children in old age*, The Policy Press, 1997

8 London Economics, *The Economics of Informal Care: a report by London Economics for Carers National Association*, 1998

9 An example of the latter approach in relation to impairment is the work of T Burchardt, *The Dynamics of Being Disabled*, CASE paper 36, February 2000

10 See note 2

11 E McLaughlin, *Social Security and Community Care: the case of the invalid care allowance*, DSS Research Report 4, 1991

12 ICA can be backdated for three months; income support, jobseeker's allowance and the tax credits can also be backdated for up to three months for special reasons (which can include being unable to pursue a claim because of caring).

13 A Hedges and A Thomas, *Making a Claim for Disability Benefits*, DSS Research Report 27, 1994

14 Carers National Association, *The True Cost of Caring: a survey of carers' lost income*, 1996

15 See note 13

16 A Corden et al, *Financial Implications of the Death of a Child*, Family Policy Studies Centre/Joseph Rowntree Foundation

17 House of Commons, *Hansard*, 6 June 2000, col 225w

18 See note 16

19 House of Commons Social Security Select Committee, *The Social Fund*, HC 232, 2001

20 See note 16

21 V Davies and C Johnson, *Moving Towards Work: the short-term impact of ONE*, DSS Research Report 140, 2001

22 J Hills and O Lelkes, 'Social Security, Selective Universalism and Patchwork Redistribution', in *British Social Attitudes 16th report, 1999/2000*, National Centre for Social Research, 1999

23 M Howard, *Public Attitudes on the Future of Welfare: research findings*, Fabian Society/Swiss Life, 1998

24 S Becker, 'Carers and Indicators of Vulnerability to Social Exclusion', *Benefits* 28, April/May 2000

25 E Holzhausen and V Pearlman, *Caring on the Breadline: the financial implications of Caring*, Carers National Association, 2000

26 See note 11; H Arksey et al, *Carers' Needs and the Carers Act: an evaluation of the process and outcomes of assessment*, SPRU, 2000; M Henwood, *Ignored and Invisible*, Carers National Association, 1998

27 C Glendinning and E McLaughlin, *Paying for Care: lessons from Europe*, Social Security Advisory Committee Research Report 5, HMSO, 1993

28 See note 11

29 See note 8

30 See note 8

31 M Hirst and S Hutton, 'Informal Care Over Time', *Benefits* 28, April/May 2000

32 See note 11

33 See note 25

34 Carers UK quote

35 Bereavement benefits replaced widows' benefits from April 2001.

36 Scottish Executive, *Consultation by the Scottish Executive on Proposals for New Laws to Help Carers*, 2001

5 Young and younger carers

GRAHAM – A YOUNG CARER

Graham is 16 and lives in council accommodation with his mother and 13-year-old sister. His father left three years ago. Graham's mother has myasthenia gravis and diabetes, and may also have cancer. She is very weak and cannot walk far. Graham empties his mother's commode, helps with the housework, collects her benefit, does most of the cooking, lifts his mother out of her chair and in and out of the bath when she is feeling very weak and sometimes washes her hair. He also helps her monitor her blood sugar level. Graham is currently in further education doing plastering but has no independent income. His mother receives income support and gives him money when she can. She is in rent arrears.[1]

This chapter covers children and young people who undertake activities to support another person (often a parent). Many policy makers define young carers as those under age 18. However, most legislation and access to benefits begins at age 16. In this chapter, the term 'young carers' is used for those under age 16. Those over 16 are descibed as 'younger carers'. Between 20,000–50,000 children and young people under age 18 could be providing care to another family member – often a parent.[2] However, different sources of information use different age bands; for example the *Family Resources Survey* collects data on carers aged 16–24:

- In 1999, 8 per cent of 16–24-year-olds were providing care for less than 20 hours a week; and 6 per cent were caring for more than 20 hours.[3]

However, there are problems with estimating numbers of carers – caring activity is often undertaken privately at home, and the definitions applied to young carers assume they are undertaking activities which children or young people generally do not do.[4] Any definitions are relative – that is, they can be affected by the age and circumstances of the child, and availability of other kinds of help. There is also a diversity of experiences – but it is often the poorest who have most difficulty in accessing services.

When the workload associated with care and assistance is high in such low-income families, when there is no surplus money to allow people to buy themselves a little leeway and when support services are thin on the ground, family members are thrown back on whatever muscle-power and personal and human resources that they can muster.[5]

YOUNG AND YOUNGER CARERS AND POVERTY

There has been concern that young people may be 'pushed' into inappropriate caring roles because of social and professional assumptions that family members will provide much of the care. This can be compounded by limited benefit payments to young people (often making them financially dependent on their families for longer periods of time) and the common experience of poverty in families where there is long-term illness or disability.[6] Such families are often headed by a lone parent and so there may be no other adult to provide care.

A study by Deardon and Becker of (largely younger) carers focussed on the experiences of 60 carers (aged between 16 and 25) who were, or had been, caring for their parents:

- Half were living in lone-parent families.
- Most families were out of work (only a third of two-parent families had a member in employment), and in most cases employment prior to becoming ill or disabled had been in manual work.
- The majority of families were living on benefit.
- The majority of parents were living in council or housing association rented housing, and a third were owner-occupiers.[7]

YOUNGER CARERS AND BENEFIT ENTITLEMENT

Social security benefits (invalid care allowance (ICA) and income support) can be available to carers from age 16. In March 2001, 3,300 carers under age 20 and 10,300 aged 20–24 received ICA, most of whom were women.[8] However, young and younger carers might not qualify for ICA because although they could be providing care for more than 35 hours a week (perhaps evenings and weekends), many are theoretically in full-time education, and so ineligible.[9] Although taking on 'adult' responsibilities, young carers (aged 16 and 17) tend to be treated as children for social security purposes, and so cannot usually receive income support in their own right (and so cannot receive the carer premium nor apply for social fund payments).

Single people and lone parents aged 16 and 17 are entitled to a personal allowance of either £31.95 or £42, the higher rate being payable to people who are living away from parents or where a disability premium is also payable. Carers of this age would therefore only be entitled to the lower rate.

Younger carers may be more reliant on means-tested benefits and experience financial hardship. Generally, young people between the age of 18 and 25 receive a lower income support personal allowance than the over-25s (£42 compared with £53.05 for single people). Only lone parents under 25 can receive a higher personal allowance. Younger carers under age 25 can, therefore, only receive the lower £42 rate.

Although relatively few carers are under the age of 25, they are more likely to be poor, as they will have had fewer opportunities to build up resources from paid employment. Young people who are caring for an elderly or disabled person could be considered as being in a similar position to lone parents, who also receive the higher rates of benefit.

Consideration should be given to examining whether younger carers aged between 18 and 25 could be eligible for the higher rate of the income support personal allowance (£52.50) alongside lone parents of that age, and whether carers aged 16 and 17 could be entitled to the higher personal allowance of £41.35 alongside those receiving a disability premium.

THE IMPACT OF CARING

As a result of their caring responsibilities, many young carers may be at a disadvantage with their education, perhaps because they cannot attend school on a regular basis, or are tired or find it difficult to concentrate when they do attend. Hence they can be at a considerable disadvantage when subsequently looking for work.

Many young and younger carers provide care without any profess-ional support, and sometimes also without other family support. A third of the families interviewed by Dearden and Becker received ongoing social care or mental health support, but another third received nothing.[10] Many cancelled services, often because of the cost.

> '[I] think it was about three or four months [home care] and then they decided you had to pay for everything...she used to go round to a day centre but it's like I think it's about £40 for two days...it was just too much for what they were doing...they're [home care] getting paid for two hours and then they're not, they're not staying for two hours.' (Kim, aged 16)

Some of the parents in the study had given up work to care for their partners; this might protect children and young people from caring roles, although this may not last if the second parent then develops an illness themselves. For example, after one parent developed back prob-lems from lifting his partner, his son became more involved in heavier domestic tasks.

Some children left home earlier than they would have chosen because of parental mental distress; of seven young people living independently, five had not planned to leave, nor was it a positive choice. In one situation the young person no longer felt able to cope with the impact of his mother's mental distress. Some young people had made 'temporary transitions', such as leaving to go to university (though often at one nearby). Others felt unable to leave because parents needed their support.

Being a carer at a young age could bring positive gains. These include greater maturity, the acquisition of life skills and practical skills (important for independent living and adulthood), and close and loving relationships with parents. However, there are also personal costs to providing care without appropriate family-centred services. The negative aspects of caring include lack of time for oneself, stress and depression, restricted social, educational and career opportunities, and impaired psychological development.

Research also suggests that young and younger carers from South Asian communities have similar needs to their White counterparts, but in addition faced racism and often culturally insensitive services.[11]

THE YOUNG CARER/DISABLED PARENT DEBATE

The recent emphasis on 'young carers' has been considered problematic because of its denial of the parental contribution made by disabled people and the contribution made by young people living in families without a person with a disability.[12] Social services departments have rarely considered disabled people as parents; a recent Social Services Inspectorate (SSI) report found that childcare teams did not necessarily record that parents had a disability, and adult services teams did not routinely record whether there were children in the family.[13]

Services have often been inflexible and not responsive to the changing needs of disabled parents because of:

- the passage of time and the changing developmental needs of children;
- the deteriorating nature of the disabled parent's impairment;
- changes in the family's circumstances.

In all of the councils visited during the inspection, some of the disabled parents and young carers did not wish to be referred to social workers, often either because they were scared that the children would be taken away or that there would be a difference of view about the appropriate level of care to be undertaken by children (though not borne out in practice).

Disability commentators have seen the increasing profile of young carers in research and policy as having a negative impact on disabled parents by ignoring the disability and the parent. As a result the development of support services, which could support disabled people in their parenting role, has been neglected.[14] There is also a danger of 'institutionalising' caring rather than preventing it from starting in the first place. Attempts to develop policy have tried to take account of these differing perspectives. Social services departments have now been told not to assume that children should take on similar levels of caring responsibilities as adults.[15] Policy guidance on the Carers and Disabled Children Act suggests that councils should ensure that the person being cared for is receiving sufficient services so that a young person of 16 or 17 is not undertaking a regular and substantial amount of caring. Authorities should also ensure that the futures of young people are not adversely affected by caring responsibilities that might undermine their own needs for education, training or work. However, there might be some circumstances (such as caring for a terminally ill parent) when the young person should be eligible for services.

In the next chapter, the position of parent carers is considered.

NOTES

1 Example from C Dearden and S Becker, *Growing Up Caring: vulnerability and transition to adulthood – young carers' experiences*, National Youth Agency/Joseph Rowntree Foundation, 2001

2 HM Government, *Caring about Carers: a national strategy for carers*, 1999

3 Department of Social Security, *Family Resources Survey*, Great Britain, 1997–98, 1999

4 J Read, *Young Carers: Back to the Future? Setting the scene: the development of policy practice and legislation*, paper to seminar 4, April 2001

5 See note 4

6 See note 1

7 See note 1

8 Department of Social Security, ASD, *Disability Living Allowance, Attendance Allowance and Invalid Care Allowance: disability, care and mobility quarterly statistical enquiry, February 2001*, July 2001

9 J Aldridge and S Becker, 'Excluding Children Who Care', *Benefits* 7, April/May 1993

10 See note 1

11 R Shah and C Hatton, *Caring Alone: young carers in South Asian communities*, Barnardo's, 1999

12 See for example, W Ahmad, *Ethnicity, Disability and Chronic Illness*, OUP, 2000

13 S Goodinge, *A Jigsaw of Services: inspection of services to support disabled adults in their parenting role*, SSI/DoH, 2000

14 For discussion see note 4

15 Department of Health, *A Practitioner's Guide to Carers' Assessments under the Carers and Disabled Children Act 2000*, 2000

6 Parent carers

MRS SHAH – A PARENT CARING FOR A DISABLED CHILD

Joy Shah is nine. Her birth was extremely premature, and for some months her continued survival was in doubt. She has cerebral palsy, with almost complete loss of mobility. She spends most of her time in a lying position, or sitting propped up. She is doubly incontinent. Her sight, hearing and speech are unimpaired, as are her mental faculties, so she is able to attend an integrated school. She is cared for by both her parents, although her mother is the primary carer.

Her mother says:

'I only think about now and what has to be done, like, tomorrow or what appointments there are and getting Joy to school and so on and concentrating on that. So, I can't think about the future but about now, what is best for Joy now.'[1]

Fourteen per cent of carers are looking after a disabled child or young adult.

Almost 500,000 children and young people in the UK have some form or disability and/or long-term illness, of which 170,000 have severe disability.[2] Each year 7,000 families learn that their newborn child has a serious disabling illness. Disabled children are more likely to live in lone-parent families, a tendency that increases where there is more than one disabled child.

Someone caring for a severely disabled child may have to spend a considerable period of their life caring, though perhaps with term-time breaks if the child is in residential school.

A re-analysis of the disability surveys carried out in the late 1980s has revealed associations between poor health/disability and socio-economic disadvantage. Of children living at home, those with a father in an unskilled manual occupation were more than three times more likely to have a disability than children born to professional fathers.[3]

A more recent survey of low-income families also found that:

- one third of couples had at least one child with ill-health or disability and 9 per cent had more than one such child;
- 32 per cent of lone parents had one child with ill-health or disability, and 7 per cent had more than one such child.[4]

Around 17,000 families in the UK have more than one disabled child, and about 7,500 have two or more children with an impairment.[5] They often have more disadvantages than families with only one disabled child:

- Parents are less likely to be in work, as most families need two carers to manage the simultaneous demands and support needs of their children.
- Most families rely on benefits but find these inadequate to meet the extra costs of having two or more disabled children.
- Parents are more likely to have a long-term illness themselves.
- Lone-parent families are more likely to have more than one disabled child.

JAN – CARER OF TWO DISABLED CHILDREN

Jamie is 13 and Jack is 7. Both are on the autistic spectrum and have severe language disorders. Being autistic means they have very little consideration for the feelings of others and means cooking two separate meals (as they are both rigid about what they will eat). Jamie is at school 40 miles away (a weekly boarder) and Jack is at school ten miles in the opposite direction. Jan visits Jamie every other Wednesday and has a babysitter for Jack – looking after one child is OK but looking after two (such as at weekends and in school holidays) can be quite a daunting task for some people. Social services treat each boy as an individual but as they do not have severe learning difficulties they do not fall into the criteria for respite.[6]

Guidance in the *Framework for the Assessment of Children in Need and their Families* emphasises the importance of a holistic assessment of family needs and the avoidance of piecemeal, repetitive or parallel assessments.

PARENT CARERS AND POVERTY

Parent carers tend to have lower incomes as they are less likely to be in work, and also incur additional costs related to their child's impairment:

- In the early 1990s, families with a child with a long-term illness were estimated to have received a gross income of over £8,000 a year less than other families with children, without taking into account any additional costs.[7] As noted in Chapter 2, households with a disabled child tend to be in the bottom two-fifths of the income distribution.[8]
- In 1998 a study of spending on disabled children suggested that the costs of bringing up a disabled child could be three times higher than a non-disabled child.[9] The second report of that study in 2001 indicated that parents spent less on items like clothing and laundry than was considered essential; the largest spending shortfall was in families where the child was under the age of five.[10]

One carer told Carers UK (previously Carers National Association):

> 'I struggle to buy clothes and good food for my other two children as all our money goes on extra heating, extra toiletries, etc for my disabled child.'[11]

A national survey of parents caring for disabled children in 1995 found that:

- parents were less likely to work because of their caring responsibilities;
- nine out of ten lone parents and over a third of couples had no income other than benefits;
- many incurred additional costs, such as for laundry, bedding and heating;
- one third of parents said their disabled children had needs they could not meet, such as for clothing, bedding and food.[12]

A later parallel study of minority ethnic families caring for a severely disabled child found even lower incomes and higher costs than the 1995 survey of (predominately) White families:[13]

- Among two-parent families, Pakistani and Bangladeshi families had lower incomes than Black African/Caribbean and Indian families. Lone parents were three times more likely than couples to have incomes below £100 a week, and over two-thirds of Black African/Caribbean families were headed by a lone parent.

- Parents reported more extra costs than the White parents, notably on food, repairs to the home, help with housework and medical consultations. Parents from minority ethnic groups also expressed higher levels of unmet need than in the 1995 study, although having a suitable home, support from the extended family and fewer children was associated with fewer unmet needs.
- Black African/Caribbean families were more likely to say they needed more money (91 per cent) than Indian (76 per cent), Pakistani (75 per cent) or Bangladeshi (67 per cent) parents.
- Black African/Caribbean families were more likely than other minority ethnic groups to say they needed a break from caring for their child (77 per cent) compared with 46 per cent Bangladeshi, 61 per cent Pakistani and 63 per cent Indian.

The re-analysis of the 1980s disability surveys also found that over half of households with disabled children could be defined as 'poor' in 1985 on the basis that they lacked some of the basic necessities in life because they could not afford them.[14] Thirty-five per cent were unable to afford two pairs of all-weather shoes. These proportions were higher than for all households, or households with disabled adults.

BENEFIT ENTITLEMENT

Many families are reliant on means-tested benefits: an early British Household Panel Survey analysis showed that half of all households with someone caring for a sick or disabled child received income support.[15] In recent years, the number of families on income support where the disabled child premium is in payment increased from 54,000 in November 1996 to 72,000 in November 2000 (about two-thirds of these (45,000) were lone parents).[16]

There is also evidence that some of the parents most in need fail to claim disability living allowance (DLA) for their child. A survey of children from the Family Fund database showed that, given two children with identical care needs or functional impairments, those from 'socially disadvantaged' families were frequently less likely to apply for DLA, were more frequently rejected, and when awarded benefit, received it at a lower level.[17] Socially disadvantaged families were considered to be lone parents, living in rented accommodation, having a large family and being reliant on benefits.

Studies have also indicated that parents from minority ethnic groups were even less likely than White parents to be receiving DLA and invalid care allowance; even when receiving DLA, they were less likely to be awarded the higher rates.[18] Parents who said they understood English well were more likely to be in receipt of benefits compared with those with little or no understanding. Similarly, in a study of families with conditions like sickle cell anaemia, receiving DLA often seemed dependent on the involvement of a particular worker, and so parents in the same locality were more likely to be claiming or receiving DLA, whereas others had not heard of it. Most families who had received DLA only did so after an appeal; families felt that the Department of Social Security did not understand the consequences nor the unpredictability of the condition and in some cases refusal was seen to belittle the parent's own caring role.[19]

Improvements have been made to benefits for families with disabled children, notably the above-inflation increase to the disabled child premium, the introduction of this premium into the working families' tax credit, improved vaccine damage payments, and the lowering of the age limit for the higher rate of DLA mobility component.

Parent carers are implicitly included in the Government's target to eradicate child poverty, though disabled children could be a more explicit sub-group. The proposed integrated child credit is likely to have a higher amount (credit) for children under 12 months old. The design of the new credit could take account of the needs of families caring for a disabled child, and could, for example, consider a higher level of credit for families facing the greatest financial disadvantage, such as where there is a disabled child under the age of five. Where the child is disabled, the proposed Child Trust Fund ('baby bond') could be boosted by an additional one-off state contribution.

The National Information Centre for families with disabled children needs to promote the services and benefits available and ensure that parent carers are aware of these as the needs of their child change.[20]

THE IMPACT OF CARING

Many parent carers are poor and live in poor homes. In one study, three-quarters of families with a disabled child lived in an unsuitable home (such as insufficient space, no downstairs toilet or bathroom, home or garden unsafe in some way).[21] Four out of ten families with a disabled child said that there were four or more features in their home which made it unsuitable.

Parents with disabled children are also less likely than other parents to be in work (see Chapter 3), and some of the issues raised in Chapter 7 (working-age carers) will also be of relevance to parent carers.

Getting appropriate childcare can also be a problem.

> 'I have had to cut back due to the quality of care needed (those who can deal with my son). It's more of a loss of freedom; the family is disabled by association.'[22]

The ring-fencing of £4 million in the National Childcare Strategy for disabled children, enabling more staff to be appointed, is therefore a welcome development for parent carers. [23]

Appropriate support may also be difficult for parents of a disabled child to obtain. Many have found that they have been dealt with insensitively, or were always being assessed; some felt that they were being 'stigmatised' by being labelled as the family with a particular condition, the inevitable focus being the impairment, to the detriment of a holistic view of the family's needs.[24] Parent carers are both parents and carers, and support services need to take account of both roles.

> 'To sit in office after office and listen to doctors, social workers, all of them, talk about me and my child as if we weren't real. We have feelings. They should remember that we are mums, that's all they have to do'.[25]

The next chapter examines the impact of caring on working-age carers.

NOTES

1 Example from S Becker and R Silburn, *We're in this Together: conversations with families in caring relationships*, Carers National Association, 1999

2 *Families with Two or More Disabled Children*, Contact A Family Factsheet, 2001

3 D Gordon et al, *Disabled Children in Britain: a re-analysis of the OPCS Disability Survey*, The Stationery Office, 2000

4 A Marsh et al, *Low-income Families in Britain: work welfare and social security in 1999*, DSS Research Report 138, Corporate Document Services, 2001

5 R Tozer, *At the Double: supporting families with two or more severely disabled children*, National Children's Bureau, 1999

6 See note 2

7 See note 3

8 Department of Social Security, *Households Below Average Incomes* 1994/95 to 1999/00, July 2001

9 B Dobson and S Middleton, *Paying to Care: the cost of childhood disability*, Joseph Rowntree Foundation, 1998

10 B Dobson et al, *The Impact of Childhood Disability on Family Life*, Joseph Rowntree Foundation/York Publishing Service, 2001

11 Carers UK quote

12 B Beresford, *Expert Opinions: a national survey of parents caring for a severely disabled child*, The Policy Press, 1995

13 R Chamba et al, *On the Edge: minority ethnic families caring for a severely disabled child*, Joseph Rowntree Foundation/The Policy Press, 1999

14 See note 3

15 L Corti et al, *Caring and Employment*, Employment Department No 39, 1994

16 Department of Social Security, ASD, *Income Support Quarterly Statistical Enquiry, November 2000*, 2001

17 K Roberts and D Lawson, *Reaching its Target? Disability living allowance for children*, SPRU Social Policy Report No 9, 1998

18 See note 13

19 K Atkin, 'Service Support to Families Caring for a Child with Sickle Cell Disorder or Beta Thalassaemia Major: parents' perspectives', in W Ahmad (ed), *Ethnicity, Disability and Chronic Illness*, OUP, 2000

20 Proposed in Department of Health, *Valuing People: a new strategy for learning disabilities for the 21st century*, a White Paper, Cm 5086, March 2001

21 C Oldman and B Beresford, *Homes Unfit for Children: housing, disabled children and their families*, Joseph Rowntree Foundation/Community Care, 1998

22 Carers UK quote

23 See note 20

24 See for example, note 10

25 See note 10

7 Working-age carers and work

PEGGY – A WORKING-AGE SPOUSE CARER

Tom Kavanagh is 55. He was 40 when he complained of a funny feeling, as though there was a feather in his eye. MS was not finally diagnosed until two years later, by which time he had been 'invalided out' of his job as a bus driver, and his mobility was being increasingly affected. Tom's condition deteriorated rapidly after about six years, and in 1990 his wife, Peggy, gave up work to look after him full time. There has been further, severe deterioration and for the past five years Tom has been totally paralysed from the neck down. He is only able to move his head from side to side. He can speak, slowly and in a whisper, but finds this exhausting.

Peggy said that giving up work:

'was a hard thing to decide because I did like my job. But it didn't seem right that I should go out to work and leave him to cope at home by himself. So I decided to pack up my work.'

Peggy now misses the 'little things' in life:

'Now our son's left home we should be out, holidays, restaurants, not every night but once a month going for a meal. You know that's what I miss, little things like that, not being able to go to a restaurant for a meal, to go down the pub.'[1]

About 15 per cent of all people at work also care for someone at home.[2] A recent Labour Force Survey analysis of working-age adults who were classified as 'economically inactive' because they were looking after the family or home found 2.3 million such people, mainly women (only 165,000 men).[3] Nearly half of the men were caring for a 'dependent adult relative' compared with one in ten women; women were more likely to be caring for one or more children under school age.

The 'peak age' for caring is 45–64, accounting for nearly half of carers. Compared with other adults, carers are less likely to be full-time employees, and more likely to be sick, or classified as 'other' economically inactive or working part time than other adults.

WORKING-AGE CARERS AND POVERTY

As noted above, carers of working age who have to give up work in order to provide care can encounter considerable financial difficulties. The situation of low-income working-age families with children is revealed in an analysis carried out for the Department of Social Security (DSS).[4] This highlights astonishing levels of longstanding illness and disability:

- Three out of ten lone parents and couples reported ill-health, especially in families without work (35 per cent of lone parents, 41 per cent of couples and 62 per cent of partners) – hence a quarter of non-working couples contained both a respondent and partner who were not looking for work.

Not surprisingly, many of these families also provided care:

- Twenty-six per cent of workless couples cared for someone other than their own children because of illness or disability (79 per cent of these were caring for their partner), compared with only 10 per cent of couples with 'moderate' incomes.[5]
- Forty-two per cent of workless couples who did not expect to work in the future had caring responsibilities, and 28 per cent said this would restrict any work they could do.
- Nine per cent of lone parents had additional caring responsibilities as well as looking after their own children.
- Ten per cent of non-working lone parents were caring for others (mainly outside of the household, caring for elderly parents).

In addition:

- people with health problems or caring responsibilities were more likely to spend longer periods on benefit;
- caring responsibilities and ill-health or disability were among the characteristics associated with lone parents and couples suffering severe hardship than families without caring responsibilities or poor health;

• conversely, severe hardship was rare among moderate income couples.[6]

Working-age carers responding to the Carers UK (previously Carers National Association) *Caring on the Breadline* survey felt worse off than older carers; 87 per cent of carers between ages 50 and 60 felt worse off compared with 55 per cent of those over 71.[7]

As a result, 'younger middle-aged' carers seemed to face greater difficulty than older carers in meeting the basic costs of living, having more problems paying bills, being in debt, worried about money and having to ask a friend or relative for financial assistance. One in three carers under 50 (compared with one in five of all carers) had to cut back on food. This may be due to not having the opportunity to build up savings and pension entitlements during a working life.

BENEFIT ENTITLEMENT

Caring on the Breadline also showed that younger carers were also more likely to be reliant on means-tested benefits: 48 per cent of carers under 40 received income support (compared with one in three of all carers).[8] Working-age carers, particularly those aged between 41 and 50, were more likely to attribute their changed financial circumstances to the low level of invalid care allowance (ICA).

THE IMPACT OF CARING

One of the key issues for working-age carers is that many are unable to work when providing care. The *Caring on the Breadline* survey found that seven out of ten carers under age 50, and nearly eight out of ten carers between 56 and 60, had given up work to care.[9]

When in work, carers tend to have lower incomes because of reduced hours and also lower hourly rates of pay.[10] They also tend to have poorer working conditions (for example part-time co-resident carers were less likely to have a permanent job or annual increments).[11] In one Carers UK survey, almost three-quarters said that their earnings had been affected by caring, with an average annual loss of £5,000; carers without a job had lost over £9,000.[12] Another estimate, based on an econometric analysis, suggests that being a carer can reduce wages by about 12 per cent.[13]

One carer told Carers UK:

'I now only get a quarter of what I used to earn but still have to pay bills at the same rate.'[14]

As indicated above, few carers on ICA currently combine work and caring – in 1996 fewer than 10 per cent of ICA recipients – 26,500 – also had earnings.[15] At present, caring may be more compatible with part-time than full-time work, with a work environment which can be controlled by the carer (eg, working from home) and with less intensive caring. As carers are more likely to work if they do not live with the looked-after person, this suggests that those who are caring for more than 20 hours a week are not engaged in much paid employment (see Chapter 3).

TACKLING EXCLUSION – JOBCENTRE PLUS

The Government's approach has been to adopt a more 'active' system of welfare, exemplified by the approach being piloted in the ONE areas. A new agency, Jobcentre Plus, will draw on lessons of ONE and the New Deals and will be established in October 2001 with a network of 50 pathfinder offices, delivering a single point of access to the benefit system for people of working age.[16] This offers new opportunities to promote both benefits and services for carers.

LESSONS FROM ONE

Since April 2000, carers living in the ONE pilot areas have been required to attend a work-focussed interview ('full participation' phase); failure to do so leads to disallowance of benefit. Carers may be required to attend an interview at the point of a new ICA claim, renewal or when circumstances change. Advisers are unlikely to see a large proportion of carers, as many of the clientele are likely to be jobseekers; in one early snapshot advisers saw only 38 carers out of almost 14,000 clients.[17] Of successful claims for key ONE benefits between June 1999 and March 2000 (the 'voluntary' phase), only 1 per cent was for ICA (1,301 out of a total of 102,000).[18]

The evaluation of ONE (for the voluntary phase) showed that, in both pilot and control areas, over 10 per cent of lone parents and 9 per cent of sick and disabled claimants were responsible for the care of a sick or disabled dependant, which affected the hours or type of work they could do.[19] A smaller proportion of claimants of jobseeker's allowance (JSA) in pilot areas (5 per cent), and in control areas (3 per cent), also had a caring role. There was some movement off JSA, including those intending to spend more time caring for relatives. Qualitative research on ONE showed that:

- people with caring responsibilities had already discussed the range of support available with specialist agencies, such as carer support groups, before any contact with ONE, and so their ONE involvement did not add much to their existing knowledge (save them knowing who to contact in the future);
- some people with longer-term caring responsibilities were quite clear that they did not want to work: ONE did not appear to have much impact on their attitudes.

Only 2 per cent of lone parents and 1 per cent of sick or disabled claimants refused to take part specifically because caring responsibilities prevented job search.

People who decided not to get involved with ONE prior to 'full participation' in April 2000 included those who had just given up work in order to care for someone and were unable to think of paid work at that time.[20] One carer had thought that going through ONE would mean attending weekly meetings:

> 'Well I said yes I would go, thinking it was like a one-off, but when they said it was a regular thing, I just said 'oh no! I can't...' it's just the fact that I sort of like, thought it was going to be every Wednesday from such and such to such and such and just got in a bit of a panic and thought 'how will I fit that in?' (Call centre, female, 52)

This may have been a matter of timing; for new and repeat claims, carers' main focus was to justify their need for benefit rather than work. Many respondents were unable or unwilling to consider work at the time of the interview, and for some, the work-focused interview was regarded as aiming to get them into work immediately, rather than having a wider purpose and longer-term goals, such as the carer's longer-term needs, future planning and independence.

> 'I ignored the first letter because I wasn't available for work because I was caring for my grandmother. I felt that I had nothing to benefit from at that moment, from the help with looking for work, and I also felt that the only benefit I was entitled to, I was getting.' (Basic Model, carer, male, 28)

People liked the idea of a single location and telephone claiming (which could save time and transport costs).

The experience of having a sympathetic personal adviser following a bereavement was highlighted in Chapter 4. As more carers will be brought into Jobcentre Plus for work-focussed interviews it is important that staff are trained to offer support to carers more broadly, rather than focussing on work as an immediate prospect (unless the carer is ready for work).

Jobcentre Plus advisers will be in a key position to signpost carers towards information, benefits, and services at particular points, such as a new claim or renewal. Having too much of a 'work' focus at those times could be perceived as intrusive or inappropriate, hence advisers need to emphasise support services available locally, including information about benefits and the new services for carers under the Carers and Disabled Children Act. They could also usefully point out how carers can get a break and how their benefits might be affected by any pattern of respite care.

However, carers often find the transition from caring into work a difficult one.[21] Clearly there is a key 'work-focused' role once caring ceases, recognised also in the New Deal for 50plus, so that ex-carers are helped back into paid employment as soon as possible. Some extension to ICA after caring ceases would allow some breathing space to allow time for an interview to take place (see Chapter 10). Former carers may still require support services and help with finances, as pointed out in Chapter 4. Carers who claim JSA can limit their availability for work because of their caring responsibilities, provided that they still have a reasonable prospect of finding work. However, this would not apply to former carers who would have to meet the usual conditions of entitlement (unless they have a health problem or impairment).

Consideration could be given to allowing former carers who have to claim JSA as an unemployed person a time-limited period (similar to the New Deal gateway) within which to explore various training and work options (such as through work trials). During this time access to a specialist personal adviser should be made available to guide former carers through their options.

BUILDING HUMAN CAPITAL

For those carers whose responsibilities are likely to be temporary, the requirement to have a work-focussed interview can be useful preparation for entering the labour market in the future (provided it is sensitively handled). Jobcentre Plus could help carers to build up human capital during a period of caring, and retain a focus on employment as a possible goal.

For example, over two-thirds of co-resident carers and over half of extra-resident carers have no qualifications.[22] Older carers are more likely to have no qualifications, but even in the 16–29 age group, 35 per cent of co-resident carers have no qualifications compared with 20 per cent of the general population of that age. Nearly one quarter of carers surveyed by Carers UK in 1996 stated that they had some qualifications, which were being under-used as a result of their caring responsibilities.[23] Others were worried about losing their skills and experience while being a carer, and many also thought that their age would count against them when trying to find work again.

Despite the demands of caring, some carers would welcome the opportunity to undertake some educational activity while caring. However, some courses which are not full time or not for people over 50 can exclude carers, or the costs can be prohibitive. As one carer told Carers UK:

> 'I would like to gain skills with computers but any courses I could apply for are costly and I could not manage the fees. I certainly don't wish to stay at home without a purpose in my life.'[24]

People are usually excluded from ICA if they are receiving full-time education or considered to be attending an educational establishment for more than 21 hours a week (this includes time spent in supervised study but not meal breaks or unsupervised study). A social security commissioner has held that this means only the hours spent attending an establishment should be counted.[25] Not surprisingly, only 10,000 ICA recipients were studying during 1997 so there appears to be little incentive to combine caring with study.[26]

As a way to encourage carers to develop their skills, individual learning accounts (ILAs) could be improved. The priority groups for ILAs in the early stages included those with no qualifications and in low-skilled jobs, and those seeking to return to work.[27] By 2000, every adult in Britain was entitled to open an ILA comprising a 20 per cent discount when spending £500 or more on eligible courses, and 80 per cent discounts on key courses, including computer literacy. As carers are more likely to have few qualifications or may need to develop new skills such as information technology (IT), ILAs would appear to be a useful tool for helping carers (perhaps preparing for an eventual return to work).

Given the importance of education and re-skilling for carers, ILAs could be enhanced for carers to use either while they are caring or after caring has ceased. An ILA account could be opened for a carer at the time of the first claim for ICA or income support through Jobcentre Plus. This could be kick-started by the Government's contribution and credits gained during a period of caring. Consistent with the commitment to lifelong learning and active ageing, ILAs could also be available to older carers. Being able to draw down an ILA after pension age could open up possibilities for older people to undertake creative courses or to learn skills like DIY (which could help reduce costs, eg, maintaining a house or car).

LESSONS FROM THE NEW DEALS

There has been no New Deal for carers, though carers were involved in the early stages of the New Deal for disabled people. However, carers are included in the target group for some of the other New Deals, especially the New Deal for people over age 50 and the New Deal for partners of unemployed people.

Both ICA and income support are eligible benefits for the New Deal 50plus, so that carers who have been receiving either benefit for six months or more can access the scheme immediately. Most participants in the New Deal 50plus have been male, with a third having poor health or a disability; a significant proportion also reported having, or having had, caring responsibilities, though the research does not give much detail on this group.[28]

Elements of this particular New Deal also include £25 million for information and communication technology (ICT) skills to improve employability.[29] New technology could be important for carers to facilitate information-gathering and communication. Older carers, in particular, may not have had any experience of computers in the workplace.

Part of the development fund for ICT in the New Deal for 50plus could be earmarked to encourage carers to develop ICT skills.

Since April 2001 carers have been included in the New Deal for partners if they are partners of someone who is unemployed, in receipt of income support, one of the incapacity benefits or ICA.

The New Deal for partners can make provision for childcare while someone is training for work – this could be extended to include respite care for carers.

While the New Deal for lone parents may also include someone with a disabled child, there remain gaps in New Deal provision, such as for carers who care for a disabled son or daughter into adulthood; someone caring for a parent; or someone caring who has a partner in work.

The new Jobcentre Plus agency for people of working age needs to develop services for carers which would fill some of the gaps in the New Deals, such as people caring for an adult son or daughter, parent; or a working partner.

SUBSTITUTE CARE WHILE AT WORK

Obtaining and paying for substitute care while at work is a major issue for most carers. The *Caring on the Breadline* survey suggested that the lack of alternative care, as well as its inflexibility and high cost, was one of the main barriers preventing carers combining paid work with care.[30] Another aspect of substitute care mentioned as a barrier was the sensitive area of the cared-for person's consent. This is one area of potential conflict between disabled person and carer, as discussed in Chapter 2.

Currently VAT is payable at 17.5 per cent on private home care, which increases the costs of substitute care while a carer is in paid work, reducing the disposable income of a household. Carers believe that this VAT is a tax on disability and that, as home care services are essential to daily living, they should be zero rated for VAT. The Government's intention to introduce an extra-statutory concession on VAT for privately purchased home care services is, therefore, welcome.[31] This concession may cover VAT on the employment costs to agencies providing home care. The Government could seek opportunities to reduce VAT on such services.

Help with care costs is currently quite patchy. As noted in Chapter 3, someone receiving ICA who pays someone other than a close relative[32] to care for the disabled adult or child while the carer is at work can have up to a maximum of 50 per cent of their net earnings deducted as care costs. The childcare tax credit allows 70 per cent of eligible child care costs[33] up to a maximum of £100 for one child, or £150 for two children, each week. Unlike the former childcare disregard under family credit, it is payable on top of the maximum working families' tax credit, and so will help families further up the income scale. Under current rules, the childcare tax credit will only benefit parent carers of disabled children.

Carers UK's research has found that carers could be spending their earnings paying for alternative care.

'Essex Social Services were charging £8.60 an hour for care. My employer pays £8.30 an hour.'[34]

Possible options for care costs when a carer is in work include:

- adopting the ICA rules;
- extending the working families' tax credit childcare tax credit to adults where 'approved care' is used, at a rate of 70 per cent; *or*
- extending the help provided for formal care through health and social services.

Consistent with the view in Chapter 2 that most formal care costs should be considered as a disability (rather than a caring) cost, it follows that the costs of substitute care while a carer is at work should be met largely through services or cash to the *disabled person directly*, rather than to the carer (either through tax credits or otherwise) – in effect, the third option listed above.

This could perhaps operate by extending direct payments or the system of vouchers for short breaks and respite care, as proposed in the Carers and Disabled Children Act, to situations of substitute care when the carer is in work. Assistance for *working* carers through health and social care would be consistent with the new emphasis on providing services which are tailored to individual needs which includes accommodating the needs of disabled people who want to work.[35]

This is now encapsulated in the adult services performance indicators:

- A3.0 – To ensure that people of working age who have been assessed as needing community care services are provided with those services in ways which take account of, and as far as possible, maximise their and their carers' capacity to take up, remain in or return to employment.

- A5.0 – To enable carers to care, or continue to care, for so long as they and the service user wish.[36]

The costs of substitute care should be seen as a disability cost. As social services assessment procedures should now also ask about work, the need for substitute care when the carer is at work should then be included in the care plan. The costs of substitute care should ideally be met through additional direct payments to the disabled person to buy in the extra support required, rather than via additional ICA or tax credits to the carer.

The next chapter turns to the position of carers once they reach retirement age, either beginning to care for the first time when they are older, or coping on a low income because of caring during working age.

NOTES

1 Example from S Becker and R Silburn, *We're in this Together: conversations with families in caring relationships*, Carers National Association, 1999

2 General Household Survey estimates.

3 National Statistics, 'Labour Market Spotlight', *Labour Market Trends*, April 2001

4 A Marsh et al, *Low-income Families in Britain: work, welfare and social security in 1999*, DSS Research Report 138, Corporate Document Services, 2001

5 Where one or both of a couple are working and earning up to the family credit level plus 35 per cent (but not higher than this).

6 See note 4

7 E Holzhausen and V Pearlman, *Caring on the Breadline: the financial implications of caring*, Carers National Association, 2000

8 See note 7, p14

9 See note 7

10 M Evandrou, 'Employment and Care, Paid and Unpaid Work: the socio-economic position of informal carers in Britain', 1995, in Philips (ed), 'Working Carers in Britain', cited in L Pickard, 1999, 'Policy Options for Informal Carers of Elderly People', in *With Respect to Old Age: research vol 3*, report by the Royal Commission on Long-Term Care, Cm 4192-II/3

11 M Hirst and S Hutton, 'Informal Care Over Time', *Benefits* 28, April/May 2000

12 Carers National Association, *The True Cost of Caring: a survey of carers' lost income*, CNA, 1996

13 D Madden and I Walker, *Labour Supply, Health and Caring: evidence from the UK*, University College Dublin, 1999

14 Carers UK quote

15 House of Commons, *Hansard*, 21 November 1996, col 691w

16 Department for Education and Employment, *Towards Full Employment in a Modern Society*, Cm 5084, March 2001

17 *Disability Rights Bulletin*, Winter 1999

18 Department of Social Security, ASD, *ONE Basic Model Pilot and Control Areas: analyses from the ONE evaluation database, voluntary phase 28 June 1999–31 March 2000*, National Statistics, 2000

19 H Green et al, *The First Effects of ONE: findings from survey and qualitative research with clients*, DSS Research Report 126, Corporate Document Services, 2000

20 D Cotton et al, *Why not ONE? Views of non-participants before full participation*, DSS Research Report 127, Corporate Document Services, 2000

21 Carers National Association, *Welfare to Work: carers and employment project evaluation report*

22 L Corti et al, *Caring and Employment*, Employment Department, 1994

23 See note 12

24 Carers UK quote

25 CG/4343/1998

26 House of Commons, *Hansard*, 20 February 1997, col 707w

27 HM Treasury, Pre-Budget Report, Cm 4076, 1998

28 J Kodz and J Eccles, *Evaluation of New Deal 50plus: qualitative evidence from clients: second phase*, Employment Service Research and Development Report ESR70, March 2001

29 HM Treasury, *Pre-Budget Report*, Cm 4917, 2000

30 See note 7

31 House of Commons, *Hansard*, 18 July 2001, col 213w

32 ie, either the parent, son, daughter, brother, sister or partner of the carer or disabled person.

33 Has to be 'approved childcare' – eg, registered under the Children Act.

34 See note 7

35 See for example, Department of Health Press Release 21 December 1999

36 Department of Health, *Personal Social Services Performance Assessment Framework Social Care Group*, November 1999

8 Carers over pension age

SHEILA – AN OLDER CARER

Sheila Roberts, 69, cares for her 95-year-old mother, Joan. Sheila has never married and has always lived at her parent's home. She retired nine years ago. About two years after this she noticed that Joan was becoming increasingly absent-minded and forgetful. As the dementia became more marked, Joan has needed ever-increasing support. She is now frail and very confused, needing constant care and supervision. She also has problems with bowel control.

Sheila feels she has 'lost' her mother:

'You become more and more outside of yourself and just involved with them... You really don't see it happening. It just happens as you go along, year after year, and you don't see it happening. So gradual. You think, 'Well, how did I get into this position?'[1]

One in four carers is over retirement age; about one million carers are over the age of 65, and around 500,000 of these are looking after someone aged 75 or more.[2] While not all carers over 65 are likely to be poor or have ill-health, many older carers provide substantial amounts of care and spend long periods of time caring. Of the estimated 1.7 million carers who provide care for more than 20 hours per week, some 459,000 are thought to be over 65. Older people are also more likely to be spouse carers (70 per cent over 65 and 21 per cent over 75), taking on a caring role at a time when physical and financial resources may be low.

OLDER CARERS AND POVERTY

Carers are now recognised as being among the poorest pensioners, alongside other groups like people from minority ethnic populations, persistent low earners and people with a long-term illness or disability.[3] These groups are poorer as a result of being low paid during working life, and so have limited second-tier pensions, or because of reduced benefit entitlement. As an example of the latter, carers may only have home responsibilities protection, which may reduce entitlement to the full basic pension, or the additional state earnings-related pension (SERPS).

Extra costs can be a particular problem for older carers; for example, a study of older carers looking after an adult daughter or son with cerebral palsy showed that many faced financial problems arising from additional impairment-related costs (such as heating, clothing, laundry, and special foods).[4]

The Carers UK (previously Carers National Association) *Caring on the Breadline* survey also showed that older carers were more likely to be paying for alternative care out of their savings.[5] Older carers were also more likely than younger carers to attribute their worsening finances to having to pay charges for services (45 per cent of those over age 71 blamed charges, compared with 27 per cent of carers under 40). Perhaps the need was greater if they were unable to perform as many caring tasks themselves.

BENEFIT ENTITLEMENT

Pension income (both state and private) seems to increase for individuals providing care for more than three or four years, perhaps reflecting the age at which caring is more likely to start and a preference for pension income over employment income.[6] However, taking early retirement can affect the amount of pension received (see below).

As older carers have been excluded from entitlement to invalid care allowance (ICA) if starting a period of caring when over age 65, there have been calls for some recognition (via payment) when caring at this age. Carers have told Carers UK:

'There should not be an age limit on ICA. I have cared 16 years and never been able to draw it because I am over 65 years.'

'When I applied for ICA I was told I was too old, yet I still do everything necessary for this person.'

An estimated 110,000 carers in Britain receiving retirement pensions have claimed ICA at some point.[7]

As ICA overlaps with the basic state retirement pension, once carers reach pension age if they claim retirement pension, ICA can only continue to be paid if the pension is lower than the ICA level (£41.75 in 2001/02). Older carers cannot claim both. When ICA has not been payable, the carer premium has not been payable either.

Part of the financial package for carers announced in 2000 included extending ICA to carers who are over age 65 when they claim, which is expected to benefit about 40,000 carers.[8] The overlapping benefit rules will still apply, so people over age 65 will not be able to receive *both* retirement pension and ICA. However, carers who only receive a small pension in their own right will be able to have that amount topped up to the ICA level, and carers over age 65 will, as a result of having underlying entitlement to ICA, be entitled to the carer premium with income support, housing benefit and council tax benefit.

Almost a third of respondents to the Carers UK survey who were aged between 61 and 70, and one in five of those aged over 71, also received ICA, suggesting that their pension entitlement was extremely low indeed.[9] One carer told Carers UK that she had lost her ICA when she received her retirement pension, even though the retirement pension was 44 pence a week lower than her ICA. Someone in this position should be able to receive the full amount of ICA with their pension when the new rules come into force.

However, many older carers have expressed the desire to be paid ICA *on top of* the basic retirement pension, on the basis that:

- ICA is perceived as a payment for caring and so should continue to be paid while the 'work' of caring is being undertaken, irrespective of age or retirement. As well as anecdotal information from Carers UK and other organisations, this was also the predominant view of carers in the qualitative sample of the Department of Social Security-commissioned research into ICA;[10]
- older carers are likely to face financial hardship at a time when they will be extremely unlikely to be able to increase their income through earnings and may have had expectations of more leisure in retirement. Twice as many recently retired carers than working-age carers in the recent Carers UK survey considered that their inability to claim ICA had contributed towards their worsened financial situation.[11]

Older carers could be helped by some of the Government's announced improvements and the additional proposals suggested above to help meet additional expenses. The proposed pension credit is likely to involve providing additional help for pensioners whose incomes are just above the means-tested threshold because they have a small occupational or private pension. This could be of great help to some older carers; the *Caring on the Breadline* survey indicated that 15 per cent of carers over 60 had private pensions and 40 per cent received an occupational pension.[12] However, more help may be needed for older carers.

Given that the bulk of the additional costs of caring should be seen as a disability cost, assistance with the additional expense of caring can be made indirectly through improvements to the system of help towards disability-related costs.

Rather than raising existing disability living allowance (DLA) age limits, there may be more scope to build in better support for older disabled people with the potential longer-term changes to DLA and attendance allowance (AA) (described in Chapter 9). These move away from care and mobility as the main proxies for additional costs, and open up the possibility of an extra-costs benefit without regard to the age of the recipient. The implications of this approach for carers' benefits need to be fully considered.

One specific improvement which would help the incomes of older disabled people (and also, therefore, of carers) would be to align the waiting periods for disability benefits (currently three months for DLA and six months for AA), so that older people only wait for the shorter period of three months.

THE IMPACT OF CARING

In relation to looking after someone with a learning difficulty, older family carers share many characteristics with their younger counterparts, but there are also important differences:

- They are continuing to care and getting older.
- They are more likely to be caring alone.
- They are more likely to have reduced networks.
- Their relationship to their son or daughter can be very strong and this can develop into mutual dependency.
- They have different experiences of services than younger family carers.
- They are less likely to ask for help just at the time when they might need more.[13]

As indicated above, older carers may also incur additional costs if they are unable to provide all of the care required, and so have to pay for what they cannot provide. For those caring for a spouse, there may be fewer resources to meet these extra costs as many of the disability-related benefits are currently less generous for people over pension age than for those who claim during their working lives.

WHEN CARERS REACH PENSION AGE – PROTECTING CARERS' PENSIONS

Carers who have spent time during their working life looking after a disabled person can often find that they have a lower income in retirement as a result. Carers who have not worked will have had little opportunity to build up entitlement to an occupational pension and SERPS. A personal pension may not be a viable alternative, as under current tax rules someone without an income is unable to make contributions.[14]

> A woman in her 50s, who would normally earn £15,000 a year gives up work in order to care and spends five years as a carer. She could, therefore, lose £75,000 in earnings. If a fully paid-up member of a final salary occupational pension scheme, she would find her pension reduced from £10,000 to £8,700 if this was drawn early – over £1,000 per year.[15]

The amount of occupational pension which can be lost depends on factors such as the amount of earnings foregone, the type of pension scheme and the timing of caring over a working life. Under a final salary scheme, years out of employment have a greater impact nearer retirement age, but for money purchase schemes the loss is greatest for years missed when younger.[16] Carers can be penalised for low earnings or gaps in contributions.

In the Carers UK research 49 per cent of carers had given up work to care and 56 per cent thought they missed out on pension rights.[17] One carer told Carers UK:

> 'I am unable to provide in any way for my own old age.'[18]

In order to receive a full basic retirement pension someone must have paid in, or been credited with, contributions for 90 per cent of a working life (44–49 years). Someone who retires without full contributions will have their pension reduced by 2 per cent for each missing year. People can make this up by making voluntary contributions (£6.75 per week in 2001/02).

While someone receiving ICA can be credited with national insurance contributions towards their basic state pension, credits must be received for all 52 weeks in a tax year in order to count for a full year's contribution record. If someone does not receive ICA for a full year they will not receive 52 credits. This can disadvantage people who begin caring after the beginning of the financial year.

> Jamila gave up work in March to look after her son after a car accident left him brain damaged. She claims ICA on 15 May. She will receive about 47 credits for the tax year which begins in April.[19]

Consideration could be given to awarding a 'first year credit' to top up any missing weeks for people who start a period of caring after the beginning of the financial year.

Home responsibilities protection works in a different way by reducing the qualifying years for retirement pension for people caring for 35 hours a week, for 48 weeks, and where the cared-for person receives AA/DLA. The same flexibility might also be extended to home responsibilities protection as credits.

THE STATE SECOND PENSION

The Government has included carers in its proposals for a state second pension (S2P); some carers will be eligible if they have no earnings, or any earnings are below the national insurance lower earnings limit, provided that they:

- receive ICA or have underlying entitlement to it; *or*
- are awarded home responsibilities protection because they are regularly engaged in at least 35 hours a week caring for someone who receives AA, DLA middle or higher rates or analogous benefits; *or*
- are awarded home responsibilities protection because they receive income support without needing to be available for work because of caring for a disabled person.

An estimated 400,000 carers are likely to build up entitlement to S2P from its first year.[20] The amount of S2P awarded to carers for a year will be based on the S2P accrual rate for the band of earnings between the lower earnings limit for that year to the low earnings threshold (£9,500 in 1999/2000 terms). The S2P will give an average of £1 for every year of caring.[21] However, there are some concerns about the

S2P as it will not be backdated, so it will be decades before carers fully gain from this proposal.

The S2P could be backdated to April 1999 to protect any SERPS contributions.

It has been suggested that national insurance coverage and pensions credits could be extended to those caring at different levels of intensity.[22] Should a second hours route be established for ICA or to the employment tax credit (see Chapters 9 and 10) this could form the basis for additional crediting in for pensions.

Credits for caring could also be introduced in stakeholder schemes.[23]

BETTER SERVICE DELIVERY AND THE PENSIONS SERVICE

The Pensions Service will have responsibility for both policy and operations on pensions, and will become a single point of access for all social security services for today's and tomorrow's pensioners.[24] This is an opportunity to develop services that are more proactive in tackling pensioner poverty and the poverty of older carers.

The Pensions Service could automatically visit older people (for instance, over age 75) once a year to check on entitlement to other benefits (as well as signposting to local services). Pensioners receiving AA could also be sent information about ICA and the carer premium to pass on to any carer who is looking after them. Campaigns to encourage pensioners to claim the minimum income guarantee should also focus on older carers as a priority target group.

Carers and potential carers may not have sufficient information in order to make an informed judgement about the impact on incomes in retirement if they give up work to provide care. The proposals to enable individuals to have better information about their future pensions, including integrated pensions statements, is an opportunity to offer more information about the impact of caring on income in retirement.

The proposed free health check on retirement proposed in the National Plan for the NHS could also include an assessment of entitlement to potential benefits and services – a 'health and wealth' check.

The next three chapters consider some reforms in more detail, starting with the benefit system (Chapter 9), tax credits (Chapter 10) and support services (Chapter 11).

NOTES

1 Example from S Becker and R Silburn, *We're in this Together: conversations with families in caring relationships*, Carers National Association, 1999
2 House of Commons, *Hansard*, 1 February 2000, col 562w
3 Department of Social Security, *The Changing Welfare State: pensioner incomes*, DSS Paper 2, 2000
4 V Alison and F Wright, *Still Caring: a study of older parents still caring at home for a daughter or son with cerebral palsy*, Spastics Society, undated
5 E Holzhausen and V Pearlman, *Caring on the Breadline: the financial implications of caring*, Carers National Association, 2000
6 M Hirst and S Hutton, 'Informal Care over Time', *Benefits* 28, April/May 2000
7 House of Commons, *Hansard*, 7 November 2000, col 160w
8 See note 7
9 See note 5
10 E McLaughlin, *Social Security and Community Care: the case of the invalid care allowance*, DSS Research Report 4, 1991
11 See note 5
12 See note 5
13 C Ward, *Family Matters: counting families in*, Department of Health, March 2001
14 See note 3
15 H Joshi, 'The Labour Market and Unpaid Caring: conflict and compromise', 1995, in Allen and Perkins (eds), 'The Future of Family Care for Older People', cited in L Pickard, 'Policy Options for Informal Carers of Elderly People', in *With Respect to Old Age: research vol 3*, report by the Royal Commission on Long-Term Care, Cm 4192-II/3, 1999
16 J Ginn and S Arber, 'The Pensions Cost of Caring', *Benefits* 28, April/May 2000
17 Carers National Association, *The True Cost of Caring: a survey of carers' lost income*, 1996
18 Carers UK quote
19 Example based on case on carersnet website.
20 House of Commons, *Hansard*, 20 December 1999, col 328w
21 Baroness Hollis, House of Lords debate 13 June 2000, col 1509
22 K Rake, *Delivering for Women? The next steps*, A Fawcett Occasional Paper, undated
23 See note 22
24 Department of Social Security Press Notice 00/067, 'New Pensions Organisation to Deliver Services to Older People', 15 March 2000

9 Benefit reforms

This chapter covers some of the strengths and weaknesses of benefits for carers, together with some suggestions for reform. The Government's announcement of the financial package for carers has been a welcome move, which will be of considerable benefit to many carers. However, some key issues remain to be resolved in the longer term.

THE ROLE OF INVALID CARE ALLOWANCE

Invalid care allowance (ICA) is a non-contributory, non-means-tested benefit payable to people who are providing at least 35 hours a week care to someone receiving the middle or higher rates of the disability living allowance (DLA) care component, or attendance allowance (AA), and who is not undertaking substantial amounts of work or study.

In 2001, 405,900 people received ICA, three-quarters of them women.[1] Following year-on-year increases in numbers receiving ICA during the 1980s, new claims have been falling; between 1996/97 and 2000/01 the numbers dropped from around 165,000 to 142,400.[2] Disallowances have increased from 23 per cent of new claims in 1987 to 32 per cent in 2000/01.

Research commissioned by the Department of Social Security (DSS) in 1991 showed that ICA recipients were more likely to care for disabled children and young adults, and less likely to care for spouses.[3] They were also much more likely to be younger and female, than are those providing high levels of care, because of the eligibility criteria and overlapping benefits rules. Where a carer was looking after their spouse, there was unlikely to be an earner in household.

THE STRENGTHS AND WEAKNESSES OF INVALID CARE ALLOWANCE

STRENGTHS

- Recognition of the value of caring.
- An independent income for carers.
- Payable to relatives and non–relatives equally.
- As a national scheme it does not preclude carers or disabled people from receiving services – ie, it is not a substitute for services.[4]
- Helps people to continue caring for longer – co-resident carers may be less likely to give up care if they receive ICA.[5]

WEAKNESSES

- Excludes those caring for a disabled person who does not receive a qualifying disability benefit – a major reason for disallowance.[6]
- Excludes carers where their partner, the cared-for person, or indeed the carer themselves, receives certain another benefits (the 'overlapping benefits' rule).
- Excludes first-time carers over pension age.[7]
- Paid at too low a level to adequately replace incomes, at only 60 per cent of the level of long-term contributory benefits.
- Excludes carers on modest earnings – more than £72 a week.

AN ADDITIONAL 'HOURS' ROUTE INTO INVALID CARE ALLOWANCE

In order to receive ICA, carers have to be 'regularly and substantially caring' for the disabled person. The test has to be consistent with the notion of caring as a full-time occupation, but not so high that administrators and claimants would have to examine in detail what activities constituted 'caring' and whether the minimum had been met. Hence a simple '35 hours a week' requirement is included in ICA.

Also included is a direct link with disability benefits (AA and DLA care). The purpose of this link is to concentrate on the most 'severe contingency' – ie, people who have given up work to care for a severely disabled person who needs assistance. Eligibility for ICA was not linked to the new lower rate of DLA care in 1992 as it was considered unlikely that disabled people who would qualify for the lower rate would require a 'substantial amount of care'.[8]

Non-receipt of the qualifying disability benefit has been a major reason for ICA being disallowed.[9]

PROBLEMS WITH THE DISABILITY LINK

- In effect, disabled people can act as a 'gatekeeper' to income for the carer as the disabled person must claim and receive benefit before the carer can establish entitlement to ICA.[10] Some disabled people may not wish to claim DLA or AA. This can create the kinds of tensions described in Chapter 2.

- Take-up rates for DLA and AA remain surprisingly low, with considerable scope for further claims (estimates have suggested that only between 30–50 per cent of people who are eligible take up DLA and 40–60 per cent AA).[11] DLA take-up does not reach above 80 per cent even among the most severely disabled people, hence the carers of people who are eligible but do not take up their DLA/AA entitlement cannot claim ICA, even if they are providing more than 35 hours a week care.

- A carer's entitlement to ICA can also be affected when the disabled person's circumstances change, and so their entitlement changes (for instance, a downward adjustment in DLA/AA could result in the total loss of ICA as a 'linked' benefit).

- For DLA at least, the original link between a benefit for attendance and ICA has been weakened. The original AA was intended as a benefit for 'attendance needs'. Although subsequently there has been some confusion about its role,[12] since 1992 DLA has been a more broadly-based benefit to assist with the costs of impairment. The DSS has confirmed that DLA is intended as an extra-costs benefit, and that care and mobility are only 'proxies' for that need, and do not reflect its purpose.[13] A working group of officials, disability organisations and other experts is working on a new approach based on 'activities involved in managing life' (AMLs); in the longer term this may offer scope for a more finely-graded approach to additional costs than the current system.

- The link with DLA and AA also excludes carers who nonetheless provide a substantial amount of care, perhaps to someone who only receives the lower rate of DLA care, or to more than one person.

The 'disability link' has been described as 'an unsatisfactory and 'system-led' way of deciding who should be entitled to financial support.' It was suggested that the disability link could be replaced by a more accurate way of measuring the amount of care-giving.

In the longer term there may be a case for a new carer test and perhaps to explore a more 'joined-up' and 'whole person' approach to delivering cash, care and housing, as suggested by Becker.[14] Future developments such as AMLs may also lead to a re-think of DLA/AA as qualifying benefits for ICA. However, AMLs need considerable development, and are some way from being a comprehensive and practical alternative.

In the meantime, one way forward might be to introduce a second route into ICA.

A SECOND 'HOURS' ROUTE

There could be a second 'route' into ICA, *additional* to the existing qualifying conditions. As indicated above, the hours test was designed to reflect caring as a full-time occupation, but not to the extent that a test would require a detailed examination of which activities constituted 'caring'. In order to avoid this level of detail in making fine distinctions about the *type* of care, an alternative second route could focus on the *amount* of care provided.

This route could be simply based on *number of hours* spent caring, starting from a lower threshold of 20 hours (based on the 1995 Carers Act definition) and a higher threshold of 35 hours (to keep parity with the current ICA structure). Benefit resulting from this route could be paid at two levels; a lower rate for those caring for between 20 and 35 hours, and a higher rate for those caring for more than 35 (further discussed below). Benefit could then be paid immediately the hours rule was met, without a waiting period.

The *Family Resources Survey* indicated that about 8 per cent of adults providing care did so for between 20 and 35 hours a week. They were still less likely to have an income from earnings than the average for carers (46 per cent of those caring for 20–35 hours had household earnings compared with 48 per cent of carers overall, and 61 per cent of carers caring for fewer than five hours a week).[15]

ASSESSMENT VIA SOCIAL SERVICES

As this is an alternative to the disability link, a separate system of assessment and verification would be required. For the first time, the Carers and Disabled Children Act offers the possibility of a different approach, as carers are entitled to a *separate assessment of their own needs* by social services departments, regardless of any connection with the disabled person. This presents an opportunity for assessments to be used as the basis for an additional 'second route' into ICA (retaining the disability link for other claims).

Any carer assessment undertaken under the Carers and Disabled Children Act could include prompting to ask if the carer wished to make an ICA claim. If so, an automatic 'verification slip' completed by social services and the carer, could be sent or emailed to the ICA Unit as evidence of caring. This would then leave the ICA Unit as the decision maker and the social services department as simply the verifier of hours and not directly involved in benefit decision making.

The advantage of this second route into ICA is that it would provide a similar independent verification of carer status as the qualifying disability benefit test, while at the same time preserving confidentiality (and an independent income) for the carer. It could also offer a new, lower rate of benefit for people caring for someone on the lower rate of DLA or not entitled to DLA or AA, but nonetheless needing 20 hours or more of care.

How many would wish to claim under the new route is uncertain, but could be relatively small. It could, however, have relevance as a potential identifier of carers for tax credit purposes (discussed in the next chapter).

However, there are considerable problems in the way in which social services currently operate, discussed more fully in Chapter 11, such as geographical variations, and delays in obtaining assessments and services. Therefore, any new addition to the social services role requires a fundamental shift towards a more uniform and rapid response to need, and a more proactive approach to encouraging take-up of both cash and care support.

A second 'hours' route into ICA could be created in addition to the disability link, based on number of hours spent caring and verified through a social services assessment.

THE LEVEL OF INVALID CARE ALLOWANCE

ICA has tended to go to people on low incomes, largely because of the financial loss incurred by carers as a result of their low rate of employment.[16] The Carers UK (previously Carers National Association) *Caring on the Breadline* survey showed that the vast majority of ICA recipients had given up work in order to provide care (74 per cent compared with 46 percent of non-recipients).[17] ICA recipients were also more concerned about its low level (£41.75 from April 2001) than those not receiving ICA, and were also more likely to find it harder to pay utility bills, more likely to worry about finances, and to be in debt.

The low level of ICA features as a major concern in research about carers.[18] This has led to calls for ICA to be raised to the level of retirement pension and other long-term contributory benefits. Indeed, there have also been arguments to bring ICA into the contributory benefits system, precisely to achieve this result.[19] Nonetheless, public support for making ICA contributory appears mixed, and somewhat confused. People appear to be supportive of greater contributory benefits for carers as they are recognised as making a contribution to society through caring.[20] However, this view seems to hold irrespective of whether carers give up work or began caring too early to build up a full contribution record; 71 per cent felt that benefits should be available to *all* carers. When asked what factors should affect the amount payable, half said income prior to giving up work, a quarter said any other income, and one fifth said income of other household members; one fifth felt none of these. A quarter thought benefits should only be given to carers who gave up work.

ICA was originally conceived as an explicitly *non*-contributory benefit, so as to include people who had not been in work as well as others who had had to give up a paid job in order to provide care. Social insurance is more developed in other European countries than in the UK, and to a degree a purely social insurance approach seems to be going against the grain of current policy thinking, which stresses a 'mixed economy' of welfare funding.

DIFFERENT RATES OF INVALID CARE ALLOWANCE

There has been concern that the impact of caring, particularly over a long period of time or for excessive numbers of hours a week, could be better recognised in the system. Hence another suggestion has been for *two levels of ICA* to mirror short-term and long-term national insurance benefits. This would award the lowest level of payment to all carers on a short-term basis during the first three months, and to carers giving fewer hours thereafter; and a higher rate at the basic retirement pension level to carers giving higher levels of care.[21]

Other alternatives include giving more help to those at the 'substantial' end of caring. Many carers already do more than the 35 hours a week required for ICA. A possible second route into ICA (outlined above) opens up the possibility of two levels of ICA, based on number of hours caring. This could mean, for instance, that those who provide above 20 hours a week care receive ICA at its current rate (£41.75), with the introduction of a second, higher rate for those caring for more than 35 hours, to bring them up to retirement pension levels (currently £72.50).

Carers who spend 35 hours or more a week caring tend to be least likely to have income from employment and more likely to be reliant on social security benefits.[22] The *Caring on the Breadline* survey also found that people who spent more hours caring were more likely to have given up work in order to care.[23] Indeed, many ICA recipients have been caring for more than 45 hours, with 37 per cent caring for more than 65 hours.[24] Maintaining 35 hours as a threshold for any higher rate would ensure that additional help is targeted at those who are least able to combine work and caring.

A LONG-TERM RATE OF INVALID CARE ALLOWANCE

A further option would be to add an extra payment for those carers who have been caring for extended periods of time, when hardship and exclusion is likely to increase. As many carers move in and out of that role, a structure favouring longer-term claimants might help to reduce social exclusion and the impact of being on benefit for long periods, at a point in time when resources are likely to be limited and goods are wearing out.

An appropriate length of time for a long-term rate could be after two years. In 1998, around 40,000 ICA claims ceased within the first two years.[25] Over a third (34 per cent) of carers on ICA had received it for between two and five years.[26] Based on recent caseloads, a higher payment of ICA after two years could, therefore, benefit over half of ICA recipients. A 10 per cent increase in ICA after two years could cost £40 million nationally.[27] (Five years would be an alternative threshold

– over one in five carers have received ICA for between five and ten years.)

Whatever the level of a 'long-term rate', such an option would require linking rules to ensure that short breaks (say for respite care) did not mean that someone would have to re-qualify for the long-term rate. Current rules allow for breaks of less than four weeks in any six-month period to be ignored; this may need to be extended to say eight weeks for the purposes of 'linking' for any long-term rate. An alternative approach would be to award a lump sum after two years (see also Chapter 2).

A corresponding change might also be needed to income support (IS) (see below). A further issue is that any large increase in ICA could lift people off IS, potentially resulting in the loss of full housing benefit and 'passported' benefits. Any such increase would then need to be sufficiently large to meet these additional costs.

Consideration could be given to increasing ICA levels with the intensity of caring and a higher 'long-term rate' for those caring for more than two years.

TACKLING THE OVERLAPPING BENEFITS RULE

ICA is not payable either where the carer could claim another income maintenance benefit (including retirement pension), or where a spouse or partner receives a dependant's allowance for the carer, or where the disabled person receives the severe disability premium in her/his IS.

The extent to which the overlapping benefits rules affect claims for ICA is not precisely known, although early research suggested that a third of people then receiving ICA, and a quarter of past recipients, had been affected by the overlapping benefits rule.[28] Ninety per cent of those affected by this rule had not known about it when they claimed ICA, which contributed towards subsequent feelings of resentment and bitterness, particularly when ICA was perceived as a 'payment for caring' or some kind of compensation for loss of earnings.

Carers have compared ICA negatively against AA and the former mobility allowance (now part of DLA) as well as the cost of residential care, which has been seen as the alternative to their providing care. One carer told Carers UK:

> 'It would cost £200 to £300 per week if my father was in a home. I get £154 per month and £25 IS.'[29]

This might indicate a need for more comprehensive information to carers and future carers about the role and purpose of ICA and the detailed rules on eligibility.

Jobcentre Plus, discussed in Chapter 7, provides an ideal opportunity to revise and promote information to carers about benefits, including the overlapping benefit rules, using a range of communication methods, from leaflets to websites.

THE SEVERE DISABILITY PREMIUM OVERLAP

If ICA is payable, the disabled person cannot receive the severe disability premium (SDP) with IS or another means-tested benefit.

To receive SDP:

- the disabled person must be in receipt of AA or the highest or middle rate of the DLA care component;
- the disabled person must 'live alone', ie have no 'non-dependant' aged 18 or over normally residing with them; *and*
- no one receives ICA for looking after that person.

However, if the only reason for ICA not being payable is because of overlapping benefit for the carer themselves (for instance, the carer receives incapacity benefit) the SDP can be payable to the disabled person and the carer can receive the carer premium *as well*.

SDP has been the subject of a number of legal challenges and amendments to the regulations, notably on the complicated definition of 'non-dependant'. Even so, numbers receiving the premium have increased from 334,000 in 1995 to 524,000 in 2000, largely at the lower rate (ie, for single people or where only one person in a couple qualifies).[30] Most of these (three-quarters) are aged over 60, and are single people with no dependent children.

There has been concern that the SDP rules can cause tensions between disabled people and carers (as discussed in Chapter 2), resulting in calls for the SDP to be payable alongside, and in addition to, ICA. Alternative suggestions include giving carers on IS an underlying entitlement to ICA rather than an actual payment, so that the disabled person could also receive SDP; or making home responsibilities protection more generous so that people do not lose out on contributory benefit entitlement by giving up ICA in favour of the disabled person claiming SDP.

A 'CARE' OVERLAP?

The reason given for the SDP and ICA 'overlap' is that SDP is considered to be a payment to someone living independently who needs to purchase care, and so to remove the overlap would be paying for the same need twice.[31] This implies that payment to support 'unpaid care' (ICA) overlaps with paid or formal care (SDP). However, in reality *both* may be needed; an unpaid carer may be providing more than 35 hours a week care, but the disabled person may still need to buy in assistance when the unpaid carer is unavailable. The fact that the carer premium can, in some instances, also be payable when the disabled person receives the SDP, makes the situation even more confusing.

The history of the SDP offers few clues to the way forward. It was introduced in response to pressure from disability organisations to compensate for the loss of the domestic assistance addition under the former supplementary benefit scheme.[32] In effect, the domestic assistance addition allowed a disabled person to reduce the demands and costs of undertaking domestic tasks by meeting the costs of private (but not local authority) home care, and as a result could help to release carers for other tasks involved in caring. Guidance also stipulated that the addition could also be paid where someone had to give up work in order to provide domestic help to the claimant.[33]

As a result some people argue that SDP is intended to pay for care costs. The Independent Living Fund treats SDP as a payment specifically for care; someone on IS will have to contribute half of their DLA care component but *all* of their SDP towards the costs of their personal assistance.

Others have argued that it is intended to pay for *domestic help*, especially as social services departments no longer provide such assistance, and given the condition that ICA is not in payment and so no unpaid carer is (technically) available to help with domestic tasks. The limited information available about the SDP suggests that on the whole it is not spent directly on care, but used to purchase large items of equipment which would reduce the need for care, and on general living costs.[34]

A further distinction that could be made is in the nature of SDP as a premium within IS. If someone's IS stops – including for reasons unrelated to the SDP (such as the disabled person working for more than 16 hours or having an increase in their income or savings above the limits) – their SDP also stops. Furthermore, as IS is intended as the main means-tested safety net of the benefits system, giving the SDP a separate purpose from the overall anti-poverty role of IS seems to be generating confusion.

In an attempt to resolve this conflict, there may be several options to consider.

1. One option might be to re-formulate SDP into an 'independent living premium' so that payment could be made to people who might otherwise be in residential care. This would have to be framed so as not to preclude payment of ICA to the unpaid carer, who might have a key role to play in helping to support the disabled person in the community.

2. Another option would be to re-focus SDP as an additional 'extra costs' payment. This might be achieved by stripping it out of IS and consolidating it into DLA/AA,[35] perhaps as an addition for those eligible for the higher rate of the DLA care component. The introduction of the enhanced disability premium as an addition to IS for disabled people under 60 may give further impetus to such a change as it too is focussed on the highest rate of DLA care. In this way there would be no SDP to overlap.

3. A further option could be developed from the second hours route into ICA based on hours (see above). With a two-tier payment based on hours, there could be an argument to allow the lower rate of ICA (where 20–35 hours care a week is provided) to continue in payment as well as the SDP. This would be based on the assumption that some hours of unpaid care are likely to be needed as well as paid formal care.

Consideration could be given to three options to reform the overlap between SDP and ICA, particularly Option 2 (consolidating the SDP into DLA/AA).

INCOME SUPPORT AND OPTIONS TO IMPROVE IT

Income support (IS) can be payable to carers without signing on as available for work:

- if they are receiving ICA; *or*
- if the disabled person is receiving AA or the two highest rates of the DLA care component; *or*
- for a period of up to 26 weeks after the disabled person has claimed DLA/AA.

IS is not payable if the claimant's partner is working for more than 24 hours. However, unlike most claimants who cannot remain on IS and work more than 16 hours, a carer can work *without* a limit on weekly hours.[36] Nonetheless, the disregard before benefit is reduced pound for pound gives little incentive to use this more generous provision; the recent increase from £15 to £20 in 2001 is a welcome step in the right direction but unlikely to substantially reduce the disincentive.

People on IS can receive a personal allowance and perhaps a premium. Chapter 5 included a recommendation to increase the personal allowance for carers under age 25.

On top of the personal allowance, there is an additional payment (the carer premium) included with means-tested benefits (IS, housing benefit (HB) and council tax benefit (CTB). Introduced in 1990 as part of a package of disability benefit reforms, it was expected to help 30,000 carers; 10,000 of these through IS.[37] By 1996, 159,000 people were receiving the premium with IS, 87,000 with HB and 116,000 with CTB.[38] The numbers receiving the carer premium with IS has increased considerably, now payable to 202,000 people – more than six times as many carers than the original estimates.[39]

The premium is payable to those receiving ICA or having an underlying entitlement (such as because of the overlapping benefit rules). A double payment can be made where both members of a couple meet these conditions. In November 2000, 133,000 IS recipients were also paid ICA; only a small proportion of these (12,000) were households over age 60.[40]

In 2000, 35 per cent of the carer premium recipients were in a household with a disabled person; a fifth were lone parents; and 18 per cent in a household containing someone over 60 (the rest were 'other').[41] Over half were couples or single people with no dependants in the household.

CARERS ON INCOME SUPPORT AND POVERTY

A third of carers responding to the *Caring on the Breadline* survey received IS; these carers seemed to face greater financial problems than those not receiving IS.[42] These were mainly carers under pension age and those from minority ethnic communities. IS carers were more likely to:

- have given up work to care (70 per cent compared with 55 per cent of those who did not receive IS);

- have had more difficulty paying bills;
- worry about finances; *and*
- cut back on food.

Given the evidence of poverty and hardship among carers receiving IS, there is a strong case for further increases in the carer premium, targeting resources on the poorest group of carers. In April 2001 the carer premium was increased by more than the rate of inflation (from £14.40 to £24.40) as part of the package to improve carers' finances. Someone who receives the carer premium can now earn up to £20 a week before benefit is affected. These are welcome increases, but more may be needed.

The carer premium could be further increased to give a higher rate after two years to target carers who have been caring for long periods and who are more at risk of poverty and social exclusion; or a two-tier carer premium giving a higher rate for those caring more than 35 hours a week and a lower rate for those caring for between 20 and 35 hours, reflecting the second hours route into ICA as described above.

The next chapter considers options for tax credits.

NOTES

1 Department of Social Security, ASD, *Disability Living Allowance, Attendance Allowance and Invalid Care Allowance: disability, care and mobility quarterly, statistical enquiry, February 2001*, July 2001
2 House of Commons, *Hansard*, 23 June 1999, col 365w
3 E McLaughlin, *Social Security and Community Care: the case of invalid care allowance*, DSS Research Report 4, 1991
4 C Glendinning et al, 'Paying for Long-term Care: a comparative perspective', in 'Ageing and Society', 17, 1999, cited in L Pickard, 'Policy Options for Informal Carers of Elderly People', in *With Respect to Old Age: research vol 3*, report by the Royal Commission on Long-Term Care, Cm 4192-II/3, 1999
5 London Economics, *The Economics of Informal Care: a report by London Economics to Carers National Association*, 1998
6 E McLaughlin, 'Paying for Care in Europe: carers' income needs and the invalid care allowance in Britain', in J Twigg (ed), *Informal Care in Europe*, SPRU, 1993
7 The Government's announcement in late 2000 of an improved financial package for carers should remove this particular weakness.

8 House of Commons, *Hansard*, 9 February 1993, col 596w

9 See note 6

10 See note 3

11 P Craig and C Greenslade, *First Findings from the Disability Follow-up to the Family Resources Survey*, DSS, 1998

12 See for example, C Horton and R Berthoud, *The Attendance Allowance and the Costs of Caring*, Policy Studies Institute, 1990

13 Quoted in A Kestenbaum, *Disability-related Costs and Charges for Community Care*, Disablement Income Group, 1997

14 S Becker, *Responding to Poverty: the politics of cash and care*, Longman, 1997

15 Department of Social Security, *Family Resources Survey*, Great Britain, 1999/2000, 2001

16 See note 3

17 E Holzhausen and V Pearlman, *Caring on the Beadline: the financial implications of caring*, Carers National Association, 2000

18 See for example, note 3

19 Social Security Committee, *The Contributory Principle, 5th report, Session 1999-2000*, HC 56-I, 7 June 2000

20 T Williams et al, *Attitudes to the Welfare State and the Response to Reform*, DSS Research Report 88, 1999

21 S Baldwin and G Parker, 'Support for Informal Carers: the role of social security', in Dalley (ed), *Disability and Social Policy*, Policy Studies Institute, 1991

22 See note 15

23 See note 17

24 House of Lords, *Hansard*, 28 October 1999, col WA48

25 About half of all cessations; House of Commons, *Hansard*, 20 December 1999, col 328w

26 House of Commons, *Hansard*, 10 January 2000, col 77w

27 House of Commons, *Hansard*, 4 July 2000, col 161w

28 See note 3

29 Carers UK quote

30 Department of Social Security, ASD, *Income Support Quarterly Statistical Enquiry*, November 1999 and November 2000

31 House of Commons, *Hansard*, 31 October 1994

32 A Kestenbaum, *Disability-Related Costs and Charges for Community Care*, Disablement Income Group, 1997

33 Disability Alliance, *Disability Rights Bulletin*, Spring 1982

34 A Corden, 'A Preliminary Study of the Use of the Severe Disability Premium', unpublished report by SPRU, 1994, cited in A Kestenbaum, *Disability-Related Costs and Charges for Community Care*, Disablement Income Group, 1997

35 As suggested by K Simons, *Home, Work and Inclusion: the social policy implications of supported living and employment for people with learning disabilities*, York Publishing Services, 1998

36 C George et al, *Welfare Benefits Handbook*, 2nd edition, 2000/01, CPAG, 2000
37 House of Commons, *Hansard*, 27 November 1989, col 428
38 House of Commons, *Hansard*, 24 February 1997, col 86w
39 Department of Social Security, ASD, *Income Support Quarterly Statistical Enquiry*, November 1999 and November 2000
40 Department of Social Security, ASD, *Income Support Quarterly Statistical Enquiry*, November 2000, 2001
41 *Income Support Quarterly Statistical Enquiry* premiums by statistical group
42 See note 17

10 Tax credit reform

CURRENT TAX CREDITS FOR WORKERS

At present, no tax credit is aimed specifically at carers, although some working carers may be able to claim one of the tax credits targeted at other groups. This can be a problem when the invalid care allowance (ICA) rules about earnings can be restrictive. A recent consultation document on the next generation of tax credits includes a question about how a workable definition of 'carer' could be devised to help people who are at a disadvantage in the labour market because of caring responsibilities.[1] This recognition of carers is a welcome development and we explore some possible options for including carers in the reform of tax credits below.

PROBLEMS WITH THE INVALID CARE ALLOWANCE EARNINGS RULES

Carers who wish to combine work and caring only have the option of remaining on ICA with low earnings. The earnings limit (raised from £50 to £72 a week from April 2001) has restricted the amount of work a carer could do while remaining on ICA. A recent survey by Carers UK (previously Carers National Association) showed that one unintended result of the minimum wage has been to push some carers out of work by raising their post-minimum wage earnings above the ICA limit.[2] At the prevailing minimum wage rates for adults of £3.70, the £72 earnings limit means that carers on ICA are limited to 19 hours work a week, and, from October 2001, when the minimum wage rises to £4.10, to 18 hours a week. Carers who are working and earning within the limit before October 2001 need to be alert to the impact of the minimum wage increase on their ICA – they may have to reduce their working time by about an hour a week.

If a carer loses ICA as a result, s/he might also lose national insurance credits, affecting future benefit entitlement and, from 2002, credits for the state second pension (see Chapter 8).

Currently, there is no tax credit specifically for carers to cushion the loss of ICA at this level of earnings. Yet estimates suggest that people look to being around £40 a week better off in work than out, although the gains of working can be lower than this for some people without children and for those living in rented accommodation.[3] This is one of the reasons for the medium-term plans for tax credits (see below).

TAX CREDITS FOR OTHER WORKERS

In-work support from tax credits is currently focussed on disabled people or low-income families with children, so unless a carer fits into one of these categories, no help is given. A disabled carer could be entitled to the disabled person's tax credit (DPTC) if working for more than 16 hours, having been in receipt of one of the qualifying benefits or receiving disability living allowance. An additional premium for a disabled child is included in the calculation of the credit. The DPTC adult credit is higher than for working families.

The working families' tax credit (WFTC) may also be relevant for carers as the conditions are that someone has responsibility for children and is working for at least 16 hours a week, and has low earnings. *Lone parent carers and parent carers of disabled children* are therefore those most likely to fall within current WFTC rules. The disabled child premium was extended to the WFTC in October 2000, so giving extra assistance to parent carers.

However, carers without dependent children or a disability are currently excluded from tax credits.

The only exception to date is the new employment tax credit (ETC), payable to participants in the New Deal 50plus who find work. The New Deal 50plus was introduced in pathfinder areas in October 1999, and subsequently nationally from April 2000. Carers who have been on ICA for six months and who subsequently make a successful claim for jobseeker's allowance, income support, or incapacity benefit, will be eligible for this New Deal if they are over 50.

This ETC is, however, different from the other tax credits in that it:

- consists of two flat-rate payments: £60 a week for people in full-time work of over 30 hours and £40 for those in part-time work (between 16 and 30 hours);
- is only payable where the person's income is under £14,999 – there is no taper so incomes over £15,000 do not attract the ETC;
- does not have a capital test;
- is paid for 52 weeks.

The ETC is also not subject to tax or national insurance deductions, and is ignored in the calculation for DPTC (but not WFTC). In some ways it is more akin to the former JobMatch payments made by the former Employment Service than WFTC or DPTC. Evaluation of the ETC (about six months after it had been rolled out nationally) found that it was the most visible and attractive element of this New Deal. Personal advisers felt that one of its strengths was that it was paid to the client, not the employer, particularly as this client group were faced with the prospect of having to accept lower wages than they had previously earned.[4] Most clients were positive about the ETC helping with the costs and transition into employment. Concerns included the impact on housing benefit (as in some cases, any gain from the ETC could be offset by loss of housing benefit), and the time limit on the ETC, which could mean that someone would not be able to live on their earnings, or their job might end (this phase of the research was undertaken too soon for any outcomes to be picked up). However, it is possible that some of the impact of losing a time-limited payment could be mitigated by an active 'follow-through strategy' where advisers continue to work with clients to ensure that they progress in employment or that they consider a range of options in advance of any payment ending.

TAX CREDITS IN THE MEDIUM TERM

Longer-term changes to tax credits are due to take effect from 2003. The broad intention is to separate out child payments from those in respect of an adult.

The children's tax credit replaced the married couple's allowance from April 2001, tapered away from families with a higher-rate tax-payer. The next stage will be an integrated child credit, bringing together the different strands of support for children from income support, WFTC and the children's tax credit into a single system of support for children.[5] This will be payable to the main carer of the child, whether or not the parent is in work, and will have a common framework of assessment and payment (rather than the separate systems of income support and WFTC). Suggestions to include additional payments for younger disabled children within the integrated child credit were made in Chapter 2.

Alongside an integrated system of support for children, the principle of extending in-work help to those without children (as with DPTC and ETC) is to be further developed. This is likely to consist of an employment tax credit payable through the wage packet, which would include an adult credit similar to the WFTC credit (currently) with a higher rate for couples and with eligibility for some people starting at 30 hours a week. Such a scheme could reach some 300,000–400,000 households without children.[6] The groups to be targeted for this new credit include older people (over 50) returning to work of at least 16 hours a week (for the first 12 months). The basic working hours requirement of 16 hours a week would also remain for people with children or a disability; for others, the hours requirement would be 30 a week and only for workers aged over 25.[7] As with the ETC, some carers or former carers might be included within this group, but they are not explicitly included at this stage.

INCLUDING CARERS IN TAX CREDITS

At first glance, it might be thought that this development in tax credits policy has little of relevance for carers. For people providing a substantial amount of care, work may not be an immediate option, so the proposed employment tax credit would not apply; equally there is no 'caring costs' payment so a model similar to the integrated child payment does not appear to be relevant either. Indeed, the idea of a separate carers tax credit similar to DPTC or WFTC was dismissed by some commentators as being of no value to carers who do not work because of the intensity of the care they provide. However, as ICA performs this function, tax credits could have a different and complementary role to play.

In summary the advantages and disadvantages of including carers in a tax credit system include the following.

ADVANTAGES

- Helps more carers to combine work and caring.
- May be able to help carers stay in work as well as return to work.
- More carers protected against further financial loss in retirement.
- More 'tapering off' rather than a sudden cliff edge at a single threshold.
- Likely to help people caring for partners who are not working.

DISADVANTAGES

- Likely to be of least help to people providing a substantial amount of care, who are least likely to be do much, if any, work.
- Partner's income and other income is likely to be taken into account, so entitlement may be lost if a partner is a middle-income earner.

OBJECTIVES OF A TAX CREDIT FOR CARERS

As there is already support for people who are *unable to work* because of caring (ICA and income support), tax credits could perhaps help those who wish to combine work and caring, *as a mechanism to compensate for reduced, rather than lost, earnings.*

For instance, tax credits could assist carers who are already in employment to stay with their employer for longer, or to help carers return to work after a period of caring ceases. Helping carers to stay in work for longer would be consistent with other policy goals of retention and progression (see Chapter 3).

The piloting of the in-work benefit for people without children, earnings top-up (ETU), has not been regarded as encouraging, given the low take-up, and because most people who claimed were already in work. However, there may be lessons for future policy. In the early stages around 6 per cent of recipients said they were also caring for someone else on a daily basis.[8] The synthesis report noted that many employees who did manage to claim ETU said that it allowed them to combine work with caring for a relative, by enabling them to reduce their hours.[9] It also indicates that, especially for older people, in-work support might help people stay in work longer (ETU payments seemed to have significantly reduced the chances of leaving employment for recipients over the age of 40). Given the problems of older people returning to work once they have left the labour market, this could be an important achievement.

A tax credit could also help carers to return to work after caring has ceased, although there may be 'boundary' problems with ICA if improvements were to be made to ICA so as to help carers combine part-time work and caring.

A series of options could be considered prior to 2003, to examine and test out a variety of benefits and tax credit mechanisms, and to discuss emerging options with carers and their organisations. The approach of piloting and consultation was suggested by Carers UK in a response to the 1998 Pre-Budget Report.

Piloting could take several forms. For instance, it may be feasible to construct some alternative approaches to be tested out in a similar way to the ETU pilots, which ran from 1996 to 1999. Alternatively, computer modelling may provide the basis for devising some options. Some possible options could include:

- tapering ICA to help more carers combine work and caring;
- combining ICA with a tax credit;
- building on the existing tax credits model.

TAPERING INVALID CARE ALLOWANCE

Currently, once earnings exceed even one penny over the £72 limit, all ICA for that week can be lost. As noted above, carers who are receiving ICA and income support are also subject to the earnings disregard for income support, which reduces the latter pound for pound over £20 a week. Any changes to earnings rules therefore need to take account of the possible interactions with means-tested benefits. One possibility might be to introduce a taper on earnings above the limit, for example withdrawing ICA by 50 pence in the £1 rather than immediately losing entitlement to it.

COMBINING INVALID CARE ALLOWANCE WITH A TAX CREDIT

A further approach could be enhancing the 'tapered ICA' option by including a tax credit as the taper eats into the ICA payment. In effect this would consolidate ICA and a tax credit, blurring the distinction between the two. It might also entail two separate mechanisms (benefits and tax credits) being in payment at the same time. This approach might be of most help to people who wish to increase their hours of work while undertaking some unpaid care, rather than retaining a link with paid employment in the early stages of caring. The advantage of this approach could be in smoothing the withdrawal rate as earnings rise.

BUILDING ON TAX CREDITS

An alternative approach would be to test out the impact of including carers within the proposed ETC in advance of 2003. Initially this could perhaps be targeted at older carers (perhaps those over age 50, the same age group envisaged for the ETC) and *former* carers of this age, or to help those already in work to stay there.

A tax credit calculated in a similar way to DPTC might help carers earn more than under the ICA tapering system, though in doing so a tax credit moves towards helping people with fewer hours of caring each week rather than to those who would be eligible for ICA.

Carers could be included in the proposed ETC, with the following objectives:

- **Helping carers in paid work to retain their employment when caring starts or increases.**
- **Helping carers who may not have substantial caring responsibilities but who could combine paid work and caring with some support for their reduced earnings.**
- **Targeting older carers over age 50 who might otherwise have difficulty returning to work once they had left.** *Former* **carers returning to work after a period of caring could also be specifically targeted and included in the ETC proposals aimed at people over 50.**

However, there are two difficulties which would need to be addressed:

- How a 'carer' is to be identified for tax credits purposes, particularly if in the early stages of caring when ICA is not payable.
- The role of hours rules – ie, minimum hours of caring for ICA, but minimum hours of working for tax credits.

As tax credits are payable through the Inland Revenue, any carer test would have to be based on other definitions (rather than expecting the Revenue to make a decision itself). Hence, a carer test would have to 'piggy-back' on other definitions used in social services or social security legislation. One possibility for identifying a carer for tax credits purposes would be to adapt the approach as described above in relation to the second hours route into ICA (see Chapter 9).

A 'carer' could be identified for tax credit purposes in the same way as proposed for the second additional hours route into ICA – ie, as part of a social services assessment which could be used as an independent verification of 'caring'.

Other possibilities include a more explicit distinction between 'caring' hours and 'working' hours. To be eligible for WFTC or DPTC, someone must have worked at least 16 hours a week. In contrast, ICA rules stipulate a minimum number of hours spent caring (currently 35). There is no limit on the number of hours which can be worked while on ICA, although in practice this is limited by the earnings rule. One approach might be to allow someone who reduces their hours in paid employment to qualify for a tax credit (provided they were within the income range). At that point they would not necessarily qualify for ICA (even under the proposed second route 20-hour threshold). The difficulty at that level would be whether a carer would be considered as 'regularly and substantially engaged' in caring by social services departments. An alternative approach would be to compensate for 'working hours lost' rather than focus on 'minimum hours caring', as caring activities may amount to 35 or more over a weekend or non-traditional work hours.

The appropriate balance between working hours and caring hours within tax credits needs to be further explored, but if carers were to be included in the proposed structure of the ETC then a lower threshold (such as the 16 hours limit which will apply to disabled people and those with children) would be needed.

If carers were to be included in the ETC, the 'carer premium' could be added to the basic credit, similar to the disabled child premium in DPTC and WFTC.

The proposed ETC could include additional payments for carers, like the carer premium.

The appropriate balance between caring and working, and so whether tax credits are more appropriate than ICA, is a debate which needs to be further developed. However, there may well be a balance to be struck between the two which could be tested in practice over the next two years.

Finally, the next chapter examines improvements to support services for carers, some of the preconditions for some of the options for tax credits for carers.

NOTES

1 Inland Revenue, *New Tax Credits: supporting families, making work pay and tackling poverty*, a consultative document, July 2001

2 E Holzhausen and V Pearlman, *Caring on the Breadline: the financial implications of caring*, Carers National Association, 2000

3 HM Treasury, *Tackling Poverty and Making Work Pay – Tax Credits for the 21st Century: the modernisation of Britain's tax and benefit system*, Number Six, March 2000

4 J Atkinson, S Dewson and J Kodz, *Evaluation of New Deal 50plus: qualitative evidence from Employment Service and Benefits Agency staff: second phase*, Employment Service Research and Development Report ESR68, 2001

5 See note 3

6 See note 3

7 See note 1

8 L Finlayson et al, *The First Effects of Earnings Top-Up: interim findings from the earnings top-up evaluation*, DSS Research Report 112, Corporate Document Services, 2000

9 A Marsh, *Earnings Top-Up Evaluation: synthesis report*, DSS Research Report 135, Corporate Document Services, 2000

11   Improving services for carers

To date, health and social services authorities have had a mixed record on support for carers. There has been increasing emphasis on seeing carers as 'clients' in their own right, with the development of respite and breaks, or sitting services aimed at carers. However, with some exceptions, there have been criticisms about the quality and speed of assessments and the fragmentation between health and social services. The Department of Health White Paper on learning disability also recognises that carers should be seen as a resource, and treated as partners.

SMOOTHING OUT THE VARIABLE SERVICE

The 1995 Carers Act was a landmark in provision for carers, but does not seem to have worked as effectively as it should. A Social Services Inspectorate report in 1998 noted that services for carers were often a lottery and often no information was made available.[1] How people are treated and the support they receive has often been a matter of chance, varying between individual workers and teams. In particular, the needs of minority ethnic carers are rarely met and assessments and reviews rarely routine. Carers UK (previously Carers National Association) has further contended that had adequate funding been available, the implementation of the Act would have been broader and local authorities freer to develop innovative responses; the lack of co-ordination with health services has also had a negative impact on carers' ability to provide care.[2]

Authorities may, therefore, need to take on a more proactive role in relation to carers. The development of national service frameworks as well as the new Carers and Disabled Children Act should generate further pressure for this lottery to end. The anti-discrimination emphasis of Article 14 of the Human Rights Act, discussed below, may also exert a more universal approach.

The aim should be for each authority to provide the same service as those held up as delivering good practice. Several mechanisms might facilitate this:

- Under the performance assessment framework for social services, performance indicators are already being developed, including carers' assessments and whether a carer received help quickly. Data on which performance is to be assessed is expected to be derived from user and client satisfaction surveys and available from October 2001.[3] Rather than simply considering the number of carers receiving an assessment as a proportion of all client and carer assessments, this indicator could also include numbers and proportion of all carers in the locality receiving an assessment, which would require councils to collect baseline information about carers. The White Paper on learning disability also suggests that another performance indicator should be the percentage of carers over age 70 for whom a plan is agreed.[4]

- Local authority funding mechanisms include standard spending assessments. These are based on a formula for each authority for each major service area (such as social services). The current formula includes information about the population, social structure and other characteristics, but is being revised. Any new formula should include additional weighting for carers, to reflect the value of unpaid caring as well as the additional support which may be required.

- Beacon status has been granted to some councils to develop as 'centres of excellence' for particular themes. One of the themes in the latest round is 'independent living for older people'. In future rounds, the theme of 'supporting carers' could be included. Similarly local 'public services agreements' could be developed to include targets of relevance to carers.

A more uniform service is needed from social services departments, which could be facilitated by mechanisms such as specific performance indicators, and more funding through a revised formula weighted to reflect the value of unpaid care to a local authority and the support needed by carers.

BETTER ASSESSMENT PROCESSES

As noted in Chapter 3, many carers do not receive the support they need in their role. Only 11 per cent of young carers in a study for Carers UK had ever been assessed by social services.[5] Half of carers in contact with social services were not fully aware that an assessment had taken place, nor of its implications.[6] However, when assessed, many carers have felt positive about the process and, in one survey, half were given extra support as a result.[7] Good assessment processes are crucial in developing appropriate and quality services for carers. Research also suggests that social services departments could give better explanations and involve the carer more in the assessment process, including giving carers confirmation of the results of an assessment as well as better follow up and regular review.

The Carers and Disabled Children Act 2000 goes beyond the 1995 Carers Act to give carers the right to an assessment of their own needs. It also gives local authorities powers to provide services to carers in their own right; allows carers direct payments for their services; and ensures that parents can receive direct payments for services to their disabled children. Services can help the person to provide care or can help to maintain the carer's own health and well-being.[8] This could include training on how to lift properly or money to replace a washing machine. This Act also needs to provide the impetus for social services and the new care trusts to develop better ways to engage with carers at both a strategic planning level and at an individual service level.

Policy and practice guidance issued by the Department of Health on implementing the 2000 Act advises practitioners to address the impact of the caring role on the individual carer; questions such as:

- Is the caring role sustainable?
- How great is the risk of the caring role becoming unsustainable?[9]

Social services departments are also advised to adopt a holistic approach that sees carers and cared-for people as partners in the caring relationship and acknowledges the abilities and contributions, as well as the needs, of all. All substantial and regular carers should have access to an assessment, and no assumption should be made that a 'main' or 'primary' carer is the only substantial and regular one. The assessment should not be seen as a test for the carer, but should focus on what outcomes the carer wants to enable her/him to be supported in their caring role and ensure that her/his own health and well-being are maintained.

USING ASSESSMENTS FOR A SECOND ROUTE INTO INVALID CARE ALLOWANCE

Carers' assessments need to be radically improved for the proposed second hours route into invalid care allowance (ICA)/tax credits (see Chapters 9 and 10) to be workable. This would require a more pro-active approach by local authorities to ensure that carers are encouraged to take up both services and cash help, and to keep delays in obtaining an assessment to a minimum so that income needs can be met as swiftly as possible. It is also likely to require authorities to ensure that carers are fully involved and understand the process and its implications (see also below). Fast-track processes would need to be developed, so that a carer assessment could be carried out within a set period. This may require tighter performance indicators. Responses would also need to be more uniform (as noted above).

In the meantime, the past neglect of welfare rights advice by social services needs to be addressed. It has been suggested that community care assessments are the point at which users need to be advised about income maximisation.[10] Becker has also suggested that carer assessments can be a mechanism to identify those most at risk of exclusion, and calls for a more 'joined-up' response to these needs, addressing both cash and care.[11] The assessment process should also include work-related help, and not assume the carer will give up work in order to provide care.

If carer assessments were to be used for verification of caring for benefits or tax credit purposes, social services departments would need to ensure that responses were uniform and proactive in identifying carers, delays were kept to a minimum and that fast-track procedures ensured an assessment within a short time, perhaps enforced by tighter performance indicators.

Carer assessments also need to be more holistic and could be used to identify carers most at risk of social exclusion; to give better information such as on welfare rights advice; to provide support to remain in or return to work.

HEALTH AND THE NHS NATIONAL PLAN

The evidence about the impact of caring on carers' physical and mental health suggests that much needs to be done to identify and support carers. A typical general practice dealing with 4,500 adults would be

likely to find 650 carers, 130 of whom would be providing care for more than 20 hours a week.[12] Though in contact with GP surgeries, none of the carers in a study of the impact of the Carers Act said that their GP or other primary care worker had told them about the legislation or that they could be assessed.[13] Some carers felt that their own health needs were overlooked. General practices will be expected to identify carers in their information systems, and should check carer's physical and emotional health whenever a suitable opportunity arises and at least once a year.[14] However, research by Carers UK found that some local carers' organisations had some difficulty in engaging staff in primary care groups, some reporting that GPs were reluctant to take on additional work, or feared that they would not be able to meet carers' needs.[15]

Carers' organisations and primary care groups need to work together to raise awareness about the health needs of carers and plans to tackle them. The Department of Health could also issue guidance about how to identify carers.

The high turnover of carers represents a challenge to health workers to provide timely support for their changing needs.[16] Some health centres have employed a carers' support worker for one day a week, who helps to identify carers, advises them on health matters as well as on a range benefits and services, and has been shown to reduce consultation rates as their needs are met.[17]

Primary care workers should be proactive about identifying and supporting carers, and offering timely support. Health centres and practices could employ carers' support workers, and implement regular checks on carers' health and well-being.

Medical confidentiality is also an issue for carers who face difficulties obtaining information about the health or care of the person they are looking after.[18] The lack of information given to carers about the needs of the disabled person is also highlighted in Carers UK research about hospital discharge. The proportion of carers who were consulted about hospital discharge dropped from 71 per cent of carers in 1998 to 64 per cent in 2001.[19] Carers from minority ethnic communities were least likely to be consulted. There has been a rise in the proportion of people being cared for who have had to go back into hospital within two months of being discharged, from 19 per cent in 1998 to 43 per cent in 2001, which many carers thought was the result of being sent home too early.

Primary care groups and hospital trusts need to ensure that carers are an integral part of the process of planning for the health and care of the disabled person and are kept fully informed and involved at all stages.

JOINT WORKING BETWEEN HEALTH AND SOCIAL CARE

One of the concerns of carers is that their needs have been fragmented between health and social care because each is organised differently.[20] Moves have already been made to encourage more joint working, such as pooled budgets under the Health Act 1999.

The National Plan for the NHS further develops the pooling of resources between health and social care, including a new range of intermediate care services as a bridge between hospital and home.[21] The Plan also includes a welcome extension to respite services, benefiting a further 75,000 carers, and the establishment of new care trusts to commission health and social care in a single organisation.

Health and social care workers have not always fully understood the needs of carers. The introduction of these care trusts reinforces the importance of greater 'carer awareness' among staff, which could be addressed through better training and awareness raising. Authorities and trusts may also want to consult with carers' organisations about the merits of other reforms such as developing specialist teams across an authority; commissioning specialist services from carers' organisations; encouraging the recruitment of carers and former carers; and the take-up of social care training and qualifications for this group.

Health and social care professionals need to be offered programmes of carer awareness and training.

Quality standards for local carer support services has already been developed, based on carers' views of 'quality'.[22] These standards can be used by any commissioning body to encourage mainstream services to be more sensitive to carers' needs; they could, for example, be adopted by the new care trusts. The five key standards are:

- information;
- providing a break;
- emotional support;

- support to care and maintain carers' own health;
- having a voice.

The NHS National Plan also proposes a single assessment process for health and social care by 2002, initially for older people. Carers need to be involved in this process.

Carers also need to be included in the process of a single assessment of older people, both as unpaid care support to someone going through this process, and in their own right as carers.

HUMAN RIGHTS IMPLICATIONS

The Human Rights Act could make a substantial difference to the way in which social services (and other organisations like care trusts) operate. Since 2 October 2000, the Act requires public authorities to act in accordance with European Convention rights from that date. Research carried out by RADAR suggests that the assessment process for community care, as well as refusal or withdrawal of services, could infringe the rights of disabled people under the Act.[23]

Some of the articles in the European Convention could be of particular importance to carers as well as to the disabled people they care for. These include Article 3 (prohibiting inhuman or degrading treatment), Article 6 (the right to a fair hearing), Article 8 (respect for private and family life) and Article 14 (the right to non-discrimination).

This could mean that, for example, a carer should be assessed within a reasonable time of making a request or being referred, and in such a way as to ensure their full and active involvement in the process and their consent at all times (Article 3). It could also mean that carers should be informed about and given the right to representation and to be heard in any complaints and appeal procedures (Article 6). And, although carers are not formally covered by anti-discrimination legislation in the same way as disabled people are by the Disability Discrimination Act, Article 14 of the Human Rights Act prohibits discrimination arising on any ground, so that a public authority treating people with like characteristics in a different way could potentially fall foul of the Act. Article 14 could also be important in 'smoothing out' some of the current variations in practice (as described above).

Rather than waiting for an individual to complain, both public services and carers' organisations need to be proactive in anticipating and negotiating how services could be better provided within the sprit of the Human Rights Act. For example, social services could anticipate the impact of the Act by consulting with user and carer groups about how each stage in the assessment process should be undertaken. The care planning stage and the actual delivery of services also need to be consistent with the European Convention. For instance, a carer's need for respite care and breaks could fall within the right to a family life, and so social services departments may want to ensure that this service is developed comprehensively and with quality.

Social services departments need to anticipate the impact of the Human Rights Act in the planning and provision of services for carers (and other groups).

The final chapter summarises the main issues and recommendations for change.

NOTES

1 Social Services Inspectorate, *A Matter of Chance for Carers? Inspection of local authority support for carers*, Department of Health, 1998

2 Carers National Association, *Response to the Green Paper on Welfare Reform, New Ambitions for our Country – a new contract for welfare*, 1998

3 Department of Health, *Social Services Performance in 1998-99; the personal social services assessment framework*, Social Care Group, 1999

4 Department of Health, *Valuing People: a new strategy for learning disability for the 21st century*, Cm 5086, March 2001

5 C Deardon and S Becker, *Young Carers in the UK: a profile*, Carers National Association, 1998

6 H Arksey et al, *Carers' Needs and the Carers Act: an evaluation of the process and outcomes of assessment*, SPRU, 2000

7 E Holzhausen, *Still Battling? The Carers Act one year on*, Carers National Association, 1997

8 Department of Health, *Carers and People with Parental Responsibility for Disabled Children: policy guidance*, 2001

9 Department of Health, *A Practitioner's Guide to Carers' Assessments under the Carers and Disabled Children Act 2000*, 2000

10 H Rainbow, 'Income Maximisation in Community Care Assessment and in Continuing Care', *Benefits 7*, April/May 1993

11 S Becker, 'Carers and Indicators of Vulnerability to Social Exclusion', *Benefits 28*, April/May 2000

12 H Arksey, 'Informal Carers Count', *Nursing Standard*, 14/4, 5 July 2000

13 See note 6

14 National Strategy for Carers, p55; original target revised to April 2002

15 Carers National Association, *Primary Care Support to Carers, practice briefing*, February 2001

16 H Arksey and M Hirst, 'Why GPs are Best Placed to Support Work of Carers', *GP*, 20 April 2001

17 H Arksey and M Hirst, 'Taking Care of the Carers', *GP*, 27 April 2001

18 See note 16

19 Carers National Association, *You Can Take Him Home Now*, 2001

20 See note 2

21 Department of Health, *The NHS Plan: a plan for investment, a plan for reform*, Cm 4818-I, July 2000

22 Department of Health, *Quality Standards for Local Carer Support Services*, 2000

23 R Fraser and G Glick, *Out of Services: a survey of social service provision for elderly and disabled people in England*, Needs Must/RADAR, 2000

12 Summary and conclusions

The evidence from surveys, statistics and case histories shows that carers are very much 'on the breadline', some spending years caring for a disabled child or spouse, often on low incomes and sharing some of the additional costs of disability. Many carers are excluded from social activities and formal support services, in some cases because they cannot afford to pay for them. Often, carers who are living in poverty have given up work in order to provide care. Large-scale surveys have also revealed a rise in the proportions of low-income families with caring responsibilities, in particular those without work, mirroring the increase in households without work during the 1990s.

As well as long-term carers, there is a surprising amount of stopping and starting of caring during any one year. This report suggests that policy needs to re-focus on these 'caring transitions' as well as supporting people who may be providing unpaid care for many years. It also indicates some options for change in the short and longer term, ranging from support to carers in their role, as well as during transitions into and out of caring.

Policies to *support* carers include the following:

- Improvements to benefits, such as higher rates and a long-term rate of invalid care allowance (ICA), and aligning the income support personal allowance for young carers with that of lone parents. There could be more support targeted on carers providing a substantial amount of care and an additional 'hours' route into ICA or tax credits via social services assessment. The overlap between the carer's ICA and the disabled person's severe disability premium could be tackled, perhaps by consolidating the latter into disability living allowance and attendance allowance. Parent carers could benefit from more explicit inclusion of disabled children in the Government's target to reduce child poverty.

- Reducing the costs associated with caring, many of which could be more properly considered as disability-related costs. This would include extending the council tax discount for carers, reducing the impact of charging for community care services, and introducing transport concessions and exemption from road tax.
- Health and social care agencies taking a more proactive role to identify carers and anticipate when unpaid care is likely to be needed (such as following a hospital stay) and offer timely support to carers.

Policies to help with the *transition into caring* include better signposting by agencies such as Jobcentre Plus, a more holistic social services assessment process which includes advice and support on finances, employment and holidays, help to carers of older people by reducing the waiting time for attendance allowance from six months to three, and an emphasis on job retention (including extending the employment tax credit for unpaid time off for emergencies and for carers over 50).

Help with the *transition out of caring* could help former carers who remain poor and excluded from employment. This could involve developing human and social capital during a period of caring (such as extending individual learning accounts and computers for carers), benefit 'run-ons' and continuing support services and specialist employment help for ex-carers, as well as a 'gateway' for former carers who need to claim jobseeker's allowance after a period of caring. There could be more pension credits for time spent caring, direct payments (to the disabled person) for substitute care while the carer is at work, using trigger points (such as registering a death) to ensure former carers are signposted to agencies providing advice and support.

MAIN RECOMMENDATIONS

The Government could extend its package of financial improvements to carers and further **tackle carer poverty** by:

- *Targeting additional help on people who provide substantial amounts of care, and for long periods*, who are more at risk of poverty and social exclusion. This could include a second 'hours' route into ICA in addition to the current disability link, based on the number of hours spent caring and verified through a social services assessment. This might give additional flexibility within carer benefits (including the carer premium) to increasing the weekly amounts with the intensity of caring (perhaps having a lower rate from 20 hours a week and a higher rate for more than 35 hours a week). In addition, a higher 'long-term rate' and/or lump-sum payments could be considered for those caring for more than two years (Chapters 9, 10 and 11).

- Helping *young and younger carers* by extending eligibility to the higher rates of the income support personal allowance, putting carers on a par with young people who are disabled or lone parents (Chapter 5).
- Helping *parent carers* by including disabled children in targets to reduce child poverty, perhaps by having an additional element in the proposed integrated child credit for disabled children under age five, similar to the additional 'baby' credit for children under 12 months (Chapter 6).
- Helping *older carers* in the longer term by improving access to disability costs benefits without reference to age, and in the short term by aligning the waiting periods for disability benefits so that older people only wait for the shorter period of three months (Chapter 8).
- *Introducing a 'health and wealth' check for older people*, building on the proposed free health check, to include an assessment of entitlement to potential benefits and services for carers and disabled people over pension age (Chapter 8).
- Helping carers of working age with their *future pensions* by awarding a 'first year credit' to top up any missing weeks for people who start a period of caring after the beginning of the financial year, backdating the state second pension to 1999 to protect SERPS contributions, and perhaps in the longer term, additional crediting in for people providing more substantial amounts of care (building on the second hours route into benefits or tax credits) (Chapter 9).
- *Tackling the tensions in the overlap between the carer's ICA and the disabled person's severe disability premium*; three options include consolidating the latter into disability living allowance and attendance allowance as an 'extra costs' benefit, reformulating the severe disability premium as an 'independent living' premium where someone would otherwise have entered residential care; or allowing payment of the premium if there was a lower rate of ICA (Chapter 9).
- *Helping carers to save* by ensuring that the Child Trust Fund and Savings Gateway for adults is flexible enough to enable carers to save when they can, without incurring any financial penalty. Where the

child is disabled, the proposed Child Trust Fund ('baby bond') could be boosted by an additional one-off state contribution. The social fund could be improved, or a lump-sum payment awarded to the poorest carers after they have been on income support for two years (Chapters 2 and 9).

- *Reducing the extra costs faced by carers.* The additional costs borne by carers are often disability-related and so should more properly be dealt with by improving assistance with disability-related costs directly. Hence the costs of meeting *substitute care* while the carer is at work or otherwise unable to provide care should be met through direct payments (or services) from social services departments to the disabled person to buy in the extra support required, rather than through mechanisms like additional benefits or tax credits paid to the carer. *The costs of additional support could be reduced,* such as by softening the impact of charges for community care support provided by social services (Chapters 2 and 3).

- Helping with the *extra costs of transport,* either by reinstating the disabled passengers scheme, or introducing a reduced level of road tax for carers, triggered by entitlement to ICA or the carer premium. Local transport concessions could be extended to include people in receipt of carer benefits or someone who has been assessed by their social services department as a carer (Chapter 2).

- *Extending council tax discounts* to people caring for disabled children, partners, or someone who receives the middle rate of the disability living allowance care component or the higher rate of attendance allowance (Chapter 2).

Local and national government and agencies could tackle the **exclusion of carers from services** through the following:

- *A more uniform service from social services departments,* which could be facilitated by mechanisms such as specific performance indicators, more funding through a revised formula weighted to reflect carers. Social services departments also need to anticipate the impact of the Human Rights Act in the planning and provision of services for carers (Chapter 11).

- *More holistic carer assessments,* also used to identify carers most at risk of social exclusion, and to give better welfare rights advice and support to remain in or return to work (including substitute care). If carer assessments were to play a wider role for benefits or tax credit purposes, social services departments would need to ensure that responses were uniform and proactive in identifying carers, delays kept to a minimum and fast-track procedures ensured an assessment within a short time, perhaps enforced by tighter performance indicators (Chapter 11).

- *Primary care groups and hospital trusts should be proactive about identifying and supporting carers*, ensuring that carers are an integral part of the process of planning for the health and care of the disabled person and offered timely support. Carers also need to be included in the process of a single assessment of older people, both as unpaid care support to someone going through this process, and in their own right as carers. Health centres and practices could employ carers' support workers, and implement regular checks on carers' health and well-being. Carers' organisations and primary care groups need to work together to raise awareness about the health needs of carers and plans to tackle them, including training and carer awareness programmes. The Department of Health could also issue guidance about how to identify carers (Chapter 11).
- Health and social care agencies need to offer *'out of hours'* support services to working carers (Chapters 3,7 and 11).

Government could build on the progress already made in setting up the carers website by providing **extra information and technology** for carers:

- Carers could be a priority group for *free computer technology* in the home, to facilitate better communication with formal service organisations and other carers in their own time (Chapters 3 and 7).
- Carers could be helped by *the provision of more information about benefits and services at key points in the lifecycle or as the disabled person's needs change*. For instance, new carers need immediate, high quality information from a variety of public services, from Jobcentre Plus, through to social services and health centres, and hospitals. Parent carers need to be made aware of benefits and services as the needs of their child change (perhaps via the National Information Centre for families with disabled children) (Chapters 3, 6 and 7).
- Jobcentre Plus advisers will be in a key position to signpost carers towards information, benefits, and local support services at particular points, such as a new claim or renewal. This could include the new services for carers under the Carers and Disabled Children Act, in particular how carers can get a break and how their benefits might be affected by any pattern of respite care. Changes in circumstances should be triggers to signpost carers for potential support, including when caring ceases – eg, when a young disabled

person leaves home or on the death of the cared-for person (Chapters 4 and 7).

- *The Pensions Service could automatically visit older people over age 75* once a year to check on entitlement to other benefits (as well as signposting to local services). Pensioners receiving disability benefits could also be sent information about carer benefits and services. Campaigns to encourage pensioners to claim the minimum income guarantee should also focus on older carers as a priority target group. Information from the Pensions Service about future pensions could include the impact of caring on income in retirement (Chapter 8).

Government could help to **tackle the employment exclusion of carers** by:

- *Encouraging employment and support services and employers* to develop and promote flexible employment practices, particularly to assist people to combine caring and paid employment. Better 'out-of-hours' services for health and support are also needed for working carers (Chapters 3 and 7).
- *Appointing specialist personal advisers for carers in Jobcentre Plus*, to assist with a 'gateway' period (similar to the New Deal for young people) for carers claiming jobseeker's allowance, and to follow through people for a period of up to 12 months back in work after a period spent caring (Chapters 3 and 7).
- *Filling the 'carer gap' in the New Deals*, so that Jobcentre Plus provides services for people caring for an adult son or daughter, parent, or a carer with a working partner. Support with childcare under the New Deal for partners could be extended to carers who need substitute or respite care; and some of the development fund under the New Deal for over-50s could be used specifically to encourage carers to develop information technology skills (Chapter 3 and 7).
- *An individual learning account* could be opened for a carer when s/he first claims benefits, kick-started by the Government's contribution and credits gained during a period of caring (Chapter 3 and 7).

The proposed **employment tax credit could be extended to carers**, with the following objectives:

- Helping carers in paid work to retain their employment when caring starts or increases, perhaps including unpaid time off in emergencies.
- Helping carers who may not have substantial caring responsibilities, but who could combine paid work and caring with some support for their reduced earnings.

- Targeting older carers over age 50 who might otherwise have difficulty returning to work once they had left. Former carers returning to work after a period of caring could also be included in the specific proposals for the employment tax credit for people over 50 (Chapters 3 and 10).

A 'carer' could be identified for tax credit purposes as part of a social services assessment, which could be used as an independent verification of 'caring' (as with the second route into benefits). A reduced hours threshold might be needed for carers as well as an additional premium (Chapter 10).

Further research could be undertaken to examine the following:

- *Caring transitions and the factors affecting spells of caring* – to deepen our understanding of the processes involved in social exclusion (Chapter 4).
- *Updating our knowledge of the financial circumstances of households* containing disabled people and carers and the distribution of resources within them (Chapters 2 and 4).

In the last Parliament, the National Strategy for Carers marked an important recognition of carers and their role. During the second term of a Labour Government, more can and must be done to tackle the poverty and social exclusion faced by many carers and to deliver support to caring relationshps.

Appendix

USEFUL ADDRESSES

Age Concern England
Astral House
1268 London Road
London SW16 4ER
020 8679 8000

Age Concern Cymru
4th Floor
1 Cathedral Road
Cardiff CF11 9SD
029 2037 1566

Age Concern Northern Ireland
3 Lower Crescent
Belfast BT7 1NR
028 9024 5729

Age Concern Scotland
113 Rose Street
Edinburgh EH2 3DT
0131 220 3345

Carers UK (formally Carers National Association)
20-25 Glasshouse Yard
London EC1A 4JT
020 7490 8818
CarersLine 0808 808 7777

Carers Scotland
91 Mitchell
Glasgow G1 3LN
0141 221 9141

Carers Northern Ireland
First Floor
11 Lower Crescent
Belfast BT7 1NR
028 9043 9843

Carers Cymru Wales
River House
Ynys Bridge Court
Gwaelod y Garth
Cardiff CF15 9SS
029 20811 370

Child Poverty Action Group
94 White Lion Street
London N1 9PF
020 7837 7979

Contact a Family
209-211 City Road
London EC1V 1JN
020 7608 8700
Freephone helpline
0808 808 3555

Crossroads
10 Regent Place
Rugby
Warwickshire CV21 2PN
01788 573 653

Crossroads Scotland
24 George's Square
Glasgow G2 1EG
0141 226 3793

Counsel and Care for the Elderly
Twyman House
16 Bonny Street
London NW1 9PG
0845 300 7585
Advice line
020 7241 8555

Department for Work and Pensions (formerly the Department of Social Security)
Disability Benefits Unit
Warbreck House
Warbreck Hill Road
Blackpool
Lancashire FY2 0YE
0845 712 3456
0845 722 4433 (Type talk only)

Invalid Care Allowance Unit
Palatine House
Lancaster Road
Preston
Lancashire PR1 1HB
01253 856123

Benefits Enquiry Line
(England, Scotland and Wales)
0800 882200
Textphone (England, Scotland and Wales) 0800 243355

Benefit Enquiry Line
(Northern Ireland) 0800 220674
Textphone (Northern Ireland)
0800 243787

Department of Health
Public Enquiry Office
Room 320
Richmond House
79 Whitehall
London SW1A 2NL
020 7210 4850

DIAL UK
St Catherine's
Tickhill Road
Doncaster DN4 8QN
01302 310123

**Disabled Living Centres
Council**
1 Redbank House
4 St Chad's Street
Manchester M8 8QA
0161 834 1044

Family Welfare Association
501-505 Kingsland Road
London E8 4AU
020 7254 6251

Help the Aged
Information Department
207- 221Pentonville Road
London N1 9UZ
020 7278 1114

**National Association of
Citizens Advice Bureaux**
115-123 Pentonville Road
London N1 9LZ
020 7833 7000

**Princess Royal Trust for
Carers**
142 Minories
London EC3N 1LB
020 7480 7788

www. homeoffice

adoption visas.

— o —